Fourteenth Annual Report
of the
Bureau of Labor Statistics
of the
State of Connecticut
for the
Year Ending November 30, 1898

Elibron Classics
www.elibron.com

Elibron Classics series.

ISBN 0-543-91222-1 (paperback)
ISBN 0-543-91221-3 (hardcover)

This Elibron Classics Replica Edition is an unabridged facsimile of the edition published in 1898 by Press of the Bulletin Co., Norwich, Conn.

FOURTEENTH ANNUAL REPORT

OF THE

BUREAU OF LABOR STATISTICS

OF THE

STATE OF CONNECTICUT,

FOR THE

YEAR ENDING NOVEMBER 30, 1898.

PRINTED BY ORDER OF THE GENERAL ASSEMBLY.

NORWICH, CONN.:
PRESS OF THE BULLETIN COMPANY,
1898.

CONTENTS.

PART I.

PART II.

PART III.

PART IV.

LETTER OF TRANSMITTAL.

STATE OF CONNECTICUT,
OFFICE OF THE COMMISSIONER OF BUREAU OF LABOR STATISTICS.

HARTFORD, December 1, 1898.

To His Excellency, LORRIN A. COOKE,
Governor of Connecticut:

SIR: I have the honor to transmit herewith the Fourteenth Annual Report of the Bureau of Labor Statistics.

Very respectfully,

SAMUEL B. HORNE, *Commissioner*.

WILLIAM W. IVES, *Clerk*.

INTRODUCTION.

In presenting the Fourteenth Annual Report of the Bureau it is essential that the subjects investigated by it and the results attained, be briefly explained as a preliminary to the exposition contained in the tabulated statements to be found in the following chapters.

Much time and labor has been expended in the work of gathering and compiling the material contained in this report, and it is a source of much gratification that, as the purposes of the Bureau become better understood, the people with whom its representatives come in contact willingly render them invaluable aid in securing the necessary data for its publications. This cannot be too highly commended, and a continuance of the existing most friendly relations between all persons and the officials of the Bureau is confidently anticipated.

CURRENT WORK OF THE BUREAU.

The current work of the Bureau covered by this report includes an investigation as to the conditions of the textile industries of the State, an exhaustive statement as to organized labor and trades unions, a complete tabulated statement of the conditions of manufactures, and an abstract of recent labor legislation in this and other countries.

TEXTILES.

Part I. of the report is devoted to the subject of textiles, it being deemed a proper investigation to be undertaken when the comparative conditions of the industry are considered. The difficulties attending the gathering of the necessary material were overcome, and the tables showing the results of the investigation will be found of interest and easy of solution. When it is understood that the manufacturers of textiles, particularly of cotton goods, have been, and are in close and direct competition with producers of similar goods in the Southern States, where the prevailing conditions as to hours of labor, rates of wages, and employment of children, are so dissimilar and disadvantageous to the manufacturers of the North, it would seem that some universal plan should be devised whereby the sections of the South employing children of a tender age, and running their manufactories a longer number of hours daily than is lawful in the North, should be brought to the same standard of belief concerning the matters pertaining to the bettering of the conditions of the working men and women, as prevails in the States of New England, the textile manufacturers of which are particularly and so peculiarly affected by Southern competition which has been so forcibly shown, and has so rapidly grown in the past few years, as to seriously threaten the prosperity of such a large portion of the manufacturing and laboring classes as are affected by it.

It should be mentioned here, that the condition of affairs as above outlined, has become a matter of such great importance, and public knowledge, that movements are at this time under way, advocated and supported by manufacturers and textile workers as well, looking to the formulation and enactment of National legislation for the relief of the manufacturers of cotton and other fabrics who suffer from competition, the character of which is such as can be regulated by legislation, requiring that the same number of hours shall constitute a day's work in all sections alike.

ORGANIZED LABOR.

Part II. consists of a complete statement of the condition of organized labor in the State, the form, scope and purpose of each particular trade having a distinct organization, the hours of labor which prevail in the different trades considered, together with a statement concerning the rates of wages paid and the benefits derived from membership in trades unions and kindred organizations.

The toilers or wage-earners, as distinguished from the employers or capitalists, constitute so large a portion of the body politic as to entitle them to the special consideration of the State, and such laws as are necessary to the fullest safe-guarding of their interests should be enacted and enforced, care being taken to avoid, as far as possible, any curtailment or infringement of the absolute rights of others. An excess of zeal may, in some cases, result in the enactment of laws, ostensibly favoring the workingman, which would have the effect to hurt rather than help him, in that they might, perhaps, cause the transfer of capital and industries to other States.

Labor organizations are made necessary by the growing tendency of capital towards concentration, a condition not entirely free from danger to the interests of labor, and such organizations should have the countenance and support of the State in every legitimate effort to protect and elevate labor. It is to be regretted that sometimes the wisest counsels do not prevail in shaping the policy or directing the action of the organizations. Labor and capital should find no insurmountable difficulties in the way of harmonious and mutually profitable employment. The greatest obstacle to such a condition is found to be the unwise course of demagogues, whose counsel is, in many instances, prompted by some motive less praiseworthy than an unselfish regard for the interest of those who follow.

One fact has been impressed upon the minds of those whose official duties or business interests have brought them in close connection with the wage-earners generally, and that is, that in the great centers of population there is, in almost every branch or trade, a surplus of willing hands, and in such branches as do not require a high degree of skill and intelligence this condition is especially noticeable; in other words, the labor market is overstocked, and the demand for subsistence leads to a willingness to work at rates which often barely suffice for the actual necessaries of life. How to ameliorate this condition is a problem, the solution of which calls for the exercise of the highest degree of political wisdom.

Of the numberless questions involved in the relations between employer and employe, that of wages is the one which most frequently cause differences and disturbances of the amicable relations so essential to the best interests of both parties. The skill and muscle of the artisan are as much his capital and stock in trade as are the goods of the merchant or the money of the capitalist theirs, and he may ask such price for what he has to exchange for money as he estimates his services to be worth. The value of that which he offers is, however, fixed by the law of supply and demand, just as is the value of the merchant's goods,

The State may not, of right, interfere in any manner concerning the rate of pay at which one shall give his services and another receive them, but the conditions under which one shall work and receive his pay are fair subjects for the care and attention of the State, to the end that right and justice shall characterize the dealings of citizens, one with the other.

MANUFACTURES.

Part III. has reference to the conditions of manufactures as found to exist in the State during the current year, and closely follows the form of investigation adopted by the Bureau and published in its annual reports for the past four years. The system thus instituted has met with approval, and if continued will be of much value to statisticians in future years. Comparisons made with the facts shown in these reports from year to year are becoming an important factor in the solution of many questions arising from the constantly changing industrial conditions.

LABOR LEGISLATION.

Part IV. contains an abstract of all laws relating to labor which have become operative in this and other countries since the publication of the last report of the Bureau, and will be found of interest to legislators and others who are interested in the advancement of and improvement in the condition of the wage-earner. Many of the laws, it will be noticed, bear close relation one to the other, showing conclusively that each State is progressing toward uniformity in legislation, which accentuates the contention of many economists that uniform or universal labor laws would work the greatest measure of good for all classes.

WORK OF BUREAUS OF LABOR STATISTICS DURING 1897-8.

The following explains the work of the National Department of Labor, and the State Bureaus of Labor and Industrial Statistics, as well as that of Foreign Bureaus, which has been accomplished or was in progress during the current year. As will be seen the range of subjects investigated is wide, and the scope unlimited. The increasing number of States instituting departments of labor is sufficient evidence that the work done and good accomplished is becoming of recognized value among legislators who deem the matter of statistical knowledge worthy of consideration.

UNITED STATES BUREAU OF LABOR.—

Economic aspects of the liquor traffic (By direction of Congress). Municipal and private ownership of gas, electric light and water plants.

CALIFORNIA.—

Free employment agencies. Collection of wages. Time check system. Eight-hour day. Japanese labor. Bake-shops. Sweat-shops. Trade unions.

COLORADO.—

Industrial conditions. Labor organizations. Cost of living. Strikes and lockouts.

ILLINOIS.—

Franchises and taxation. Mine inspection. Private and municipal ownership of gas, electric light and water plants.

INDIANA.—

Industrial statistics. Mortgages and satisfactions. Railroad statistics.

IOWA.—

Employment statistics. Railroad employes' wages. Manual training schools.

KANSAS.—

Milling industry. Creamery industry. Poultry industry. General manufactures. Labor unions. Cigar industry. Packing industry. Lead and zinc mines.

KENTUCKY.—

Mineral and agricultural resources of the State. Farm products and cost of production. Coal miners' strikes.

MARYLAND.—

Industrial statistics. Iron industry. Street railways. Female labor, Sweat-shops. Employment agencies. Convict labor. Strikes and compulsory arbitration.

MAINE.—

Manufacturing statistics. Summer resorts of Maine. Manufactures in wood novelties.

MASSACHUSETTS.—

Graded weekly wages. Statistics of manufactures. Relation of intemperance to crime, pauperism and insanity. Labor chronology.

MICHIGAN.—

Manufacture of vehicles. Eight-hour workday. Penal and reformatory institutions. Strikes and lockouts.

MINNESOTA.—

Purchasing power of gold.

MISSOURI.—

Street railway franchises. Taxation of real estate. Farm mortgages. Factory inspection.

MONTANA.—

Railroad wages and traffic. Labor and employment.

NEBRASKA.—

Resources of Nebraska. Farm and industrial statistics. Mortgage indebtedness.

NEW HAMPSHIRE.—

Manufacturers' statistics. Shoe industry. Retail prices of food and fuel. Strikes and lockouts.

NEW JERSEY.—

Statistics of manufacturers. Building and loan associations. Labor legislation.

NEW YORK.—

Condition of organized labor. Progress of business in the productive industries of the State for five years. Wholesale and retail prices of meats and groceries for five years. Private and municipal ownership of gas, electric light and water plants. Wages, condition and treatment of unorganized workmen in New York City.

NORTH CAROLINA.—

Agricultural statistics. Cotton and woolen mills. Tobacco factories.

OHIO.—

Employment agencies. Clay-working industries. Coal mining statistics. Manufacturers' statistics.

PENNSYLVANIA.—

Statistics of manufacturers. Tin-plate mills in the State. Industrial time and earnings. Strikes and lockouts. Prison labor.

RHODE ISLAND.—

Statistics of manufacturers. Textile industries. Occupation by sex.

TENNESSEE.—

Mines and mine inspection. Mine wages and regulations. General labor conditions. Phosphate industry. Marble industry. Petroleum fields.

WISCONSIN.—

Cost of grain production and the relation of this cost to the value of the product. Manufacturers' statistics. Factory inspection.

FOREIGN BUREAUS.

AUSTRIA.—

Strikes by industries, percentage of strikers and days lost.

BELGIUM.—

Wages and cost of living.

FRANCE.—

Minimum wages paid to employes on public works in England, Belgium, Holland, Switzerland, United States and France.

GERMANY.—

Labor conditions of garment workers. Hours of labor, wages, health and morals.

GREAT BRITAIN.—

Trades unions in Great Britain and Ireland. Price lists and sliding scales. Changes in wages and hours of labor.

ITALY.—

Strikes and lockouts. Causes and results.

NEW ZEALAND.—

Account of accidents and legal decisions under the Factory Act. Condition of the labor market. Conciliation and arbitration. Hours of labor and wages. Report on factory inspection.

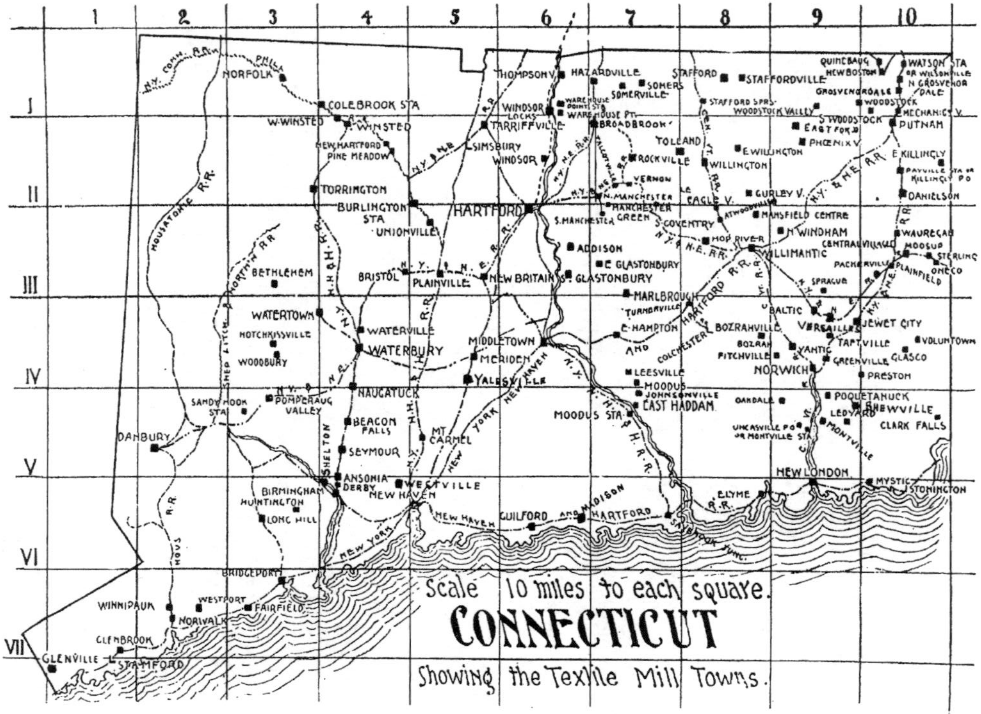

Scale 10 miles to each square.
CONNECTICUT
Showing the Textile Mill Towns.
1
2
3
4
5
6
7
8
9
10
I
II
III
IV
V
VI
VII
NORFOLK
COLEBROOK STA
W. WINSTED
WINSTED
NEW HARTFORD
PINE MEADOW
TORRINGTON
BURLINGTON STA
UNIONVILLE
THOMPSONV.
HAZARDVILLE
STAFFORD
STAFFORDVILLE
SOMERS
SOMERVILLE
WINDSOR LOCKS
WAREHOUSE PT.
BROADBROOK
TARRIFFVILLE
SIMSBURY
WINDSOR
ROCKVILLE
TOLLAND
VERNON
HARTFORD
N. MANCHESTER
MANCHESTER GREEN
S. MANCHESTER
S. COVENTRY
EAGLE V.
WILLINGTON
E. WILLINGTON
STAFFORD SPRS.
WOODSTOCK VALLEY
QUINEBAUG
NEW BOSTON
WATSON STA
N GROSVENOR DALE
GROSVENORDALE
WOODSTOCK
S. WOODSTOCK
MECHANIC V.
PUTNAM
EAST FORD
PHOENIX V.
E. KILLINGLY
DAYVILLE
KILLINGLY P.O.
DANIELSON
GURLEY V.
ATWOODVILLE
MANSFIELD CENTRE
N. WINDHAM
HOP RIVER
WILLIMANTIC
WAUREGAN
CENTRAL VILLAGE
MOOSUP
STERLING
ONECO
PLAINFIELD
PACKERVILLE
SPRAGUE
ADDISON
E. GLASTONBURY
GLASTONBURY
NEW BRITAIN
PLAINVILLE
BRISTOL
BETHLEHEM
WATERTOWN
HOTCHKISSVILLE
WOODBURY
WATERVILLE
WATERBURY
MIDDLETOWN
MERIDEN
YALESVILLE
MARLBOROUGH
TURNERVILLE
E. HAMPTON
BOZRAHVILLE
BOZRAH
FITCHVILLE
YANTIC
BALTIC
VERSAILLES
JEWETT CITY
TAFTVILLE
VOLUNTOWN
GREENVILLE
GLASCO
NORWICH
PRESTON
LEESVILLE
MOODUS
JOHNSONVILLE
EAST HADDAM
MOODUS STA.
OAKDALE
POQUETANUCK
LEDYARD
SHEWVILLE
CLARK FALLS
UNCASVILLE P.O.
OR MONTVILLE STA.
MONTVILLE
NAUGATUCK
POMPERAUG VALLEY
SANDY HOOK STA.
BEACON FALLS
SEYMOUR
MT. CARMEL
DANBURY
SHELTON
ANSONIA
DERBY
WESTVILLE
NEW HAVEN
BIRMINGHAM
HUNTINGTON
LONG HILL
GUILFORD
MADISON
HARTFORD
NEW LONDON
MYSTIC
STONINGTON
LYME
BRIDGEPORT
WESTPORT
FAIRFIELD
WINNIPAUK
NORWALK
GLENBROOK
GLENVILLE
STAMFORD
HOUSATONIC R.R.
NORTHERN R.R.
N.Y. & N.E. R.R.
HARTFORD R.R.
NEW YORK
NEW HAVEN
SAYBROOK JUNC.

PART I.

TEXTILE INDUSTRIES OF CONNECTICUT.

1. COTTON.
2. WOOLEN.
3. KNIT GOODS.
4. SILK.
5. CAPITAL.
6. NUMBER EMPLOYED.
7. WAGES.
8. LOOMS AND SPINDLES.
9. VALUE OF PRODUCT.
10. ASSESSMENTS AND TAXES.

TEXTILE INDUSTRIES OF CONNECTICUT.

COTTON.

THE depression which has prevailed throughout the country for the past five years, has most materially affected the Textile manufacturing industries of Connecticut, and it is the purpose of the Bureau to give, in this chapter of the report, as complete and exhaustive a statement of the actual condition of the manufacturing establishments of the State which are engaged in the cotton, woolen, knit goods and silk industries, as has been possible to secure.

The tables have been prepared and arranged with a view to simplicity in detail, and the results obtained will show that the desire of the Bureau for accuracy and completeness has been gratified.

The collecting of the material for this portion of the report necessitated the performance of an immense amount of labor, in order that the data secured should be of the utmost reliability, and that this has been attained is unquestionable. Much of this labor might have been saved had more of the manufacturers complied with the requests made by the Bureau, and made the returns on the blank schedules which were prepared and mailed to every manufacturer of Textiles in the State. This reluctance, on the part of the proprietors of many establishments, rendered personal visits necessary, and in some instances the special agent engaged in this work was compelled to make numerous calls and earnest solicitation in order to secure the statements required.

Some little objection was made by the proprietors of a few establishments to furnish the Bureau with a statement of the amount paid in wages, obviously fearing exposure of labor cost of product. When assured, however, that in no event was the identity of the establishment to be disclosed, the figures were obtained, and it should be here stated that the assurances thus given have been fully complied with, and the wage account as rendered does not appear separately, but in the aggregate only.

Reference should be made to the fact that the amounts given in the tables as "capital invested" is hardly a just statement, as in many cases the statements of manufacturers concerning this point was to the effect that the amount so given was "capital stock of corporation" or "original capital," and in a few cases only were the figures given stated to have included "capital and surplus". It is, therefore, safe to assume that the amount of capital actually invested in the manufacture of Textiles in Connecticut is largely in excess of the amount given in the tables as total capital invested.

The table showing the total number of spindles in operation in 1897, exhibits most accurately the capacity of the cotton mills of the State, for, while the number of working spindles is by no means an exact measure of capacity, it is most certainly the best measure. Either this, or the quantity of raw material used must be taken as a measure of capacity. Should the quantity of raw material, that is of cotton, or the superficial area or weight of the product be taken as such measure, either would be open to the fatal objection that the cheapest goods are those in the making of which the largest amount of cotton is consumed. The same fatal objection would also apply to all other manufactures of Textiles. It would appear, therefore, that the capacity for production can be most accurately determined on the basis of the number of spindles in operation.

Comparisons made with the United States Census report of 1890 develops the fact that there were 934,155 spindles in active operation in the cotton mills of Connecticut at that time. The number found to be in operation in the sixty establishments represented in the tables as manufacturers of cotton cloths, warps, webs, threads and yarns in 1897 was 1,038,020, an increase in number of spindles of 103,865, or 11 per cent.

The number of idle spindles in the State in 1890, as given in the same report, was 16,852, while in 1897 there were reported 56,048 as being idle, an increase in number of idle spindles of 39,196, or 233 per cent. The total spindle capacity in the

State, however, was in 1897, 1,094,068 (idle spindles included), while by the census figures of 1890 there were 951,007 (idle spindles included), an increase in 1897 over 1890 of 143,061, or 15 per cent.

Reference to the tables which follow this analysis will show that, as stated in the preceding paragraph, the number of spindles in operation in 1897 was 1,038,020; the number of persons employed in the sixty establishments engaged in the manufacture of cotton cloths, warps, webs, threads and yarns being 15,637, and the amount paid in wages, exclusive of salaries, $4,830,023.37. The labor cost per spindle, therefore, being $4.65, and the number of spindles operated per employe 66.38.

The number of pounds of cotton consumed in the same establishments in 1897 was 53,104,000, the consumption, therefore, being 51.16 pounds per spindle.

The thirty-one establishments represented in the tables as manufacturing cotton cloths, by which term it is intended to cover manufacturers of cotton cloths, prints, crinolines, tarletans, denims, ticks, ducks, ginghams, cambrics and satines, produced 162,067,993 yards of goods in 1897. The total value of product is stated to have been $8,487,664.51, or 5.24 per yard. The amount paid in wages, exclusive of salaries, was $3,204,131.94, or 37.8 per cent. of product value.

The per cent. of product value paid for wages in the sixty establishments referred to in the tables, when placed in comparison with the figures given in the United States Census of 1890, are interesting and instructive, for in these establishments in 1897 the total value of product, as will be seen by reference to the tables, was $15,540,534.42, and the total amount paid in wages by the same establishments for the period named was $4,830,023.37. The wages paid, therefore, being 31.1 per cent. of product value. By the use of the same method in the data drawn from the Census report, it is found that in the cotton industries of Connecticut in 1860, the per cent. wages paid of product value was 19.6; in 1870, 23.1 per cent.; in 1880, 22.6 per cent.; and in 1890, 29.4 per cent. It is obvious then, that the contention of some economists that labor is gradually but surely increasing the portion secured by it of the value of its productions, is substantiated.

As before stated, the number employed in the sixty establishments referred to in the tables as manufacturers of cotton cloths, warps, webs, threads and yarns was, in 1897, 15,637, which sub-divided, comprised 6,950 men, 7,135 women, 817 boys and 735 girls—the two latter named classes being under 16 years of age, showing that of the total number employed in these industries 9.9 per cent. were children.

In respect to the above, it might be well to compare this condition with that which exists in North Carolina, where, according to the report of the Bureau of Labor Statistics of that State, issued in 1897, there were employed in all the mills 23,435 persons, 6,046, or 25.8 per cent. of which were classified as children.

The tables which follow have been compiled with great care and the accompanying explanations will render them of much interest and value.

COTTON CLOTHS.

TABLE No. 1.—Capacity for Production.

Number of Establishment.	Capital invested.	Horse power.	Looms in operation.	Spindles in operation.	Bales of cotton used in 1897.	Average number employed during 1897.				
						Men.	Women.	Boys.	Girls.	Total.
1	$150,000	300	307	14,640	1,561	65	38	11	12	126
2	600,000	1,800	1,464	59,616	4,429	408	231	22	10	671
3	135,000	275	282	15,296	487	88	52	10	7	157
4	175,000	400	451	21,080	1,703	108	78	3	1	190
5	2,000,000	2,100	2,775	118,938	2,500	500	700	160	140	1,500
6	100,000	150	172	10,704	900	45	20	18	16	99
7	100,000	300	224	7,500	3,454	100	80	6	6	192
8	100,000	250	300	13,280	1,423	62	56	15	9	142
9	200,000	650	648	23,640	2,784	170	95	3	6	274
10	150,000	400	465	20,000	1,811	85	68	27	27	207
11	150,000	250	358	11,696	1,250	83	52	36	18	189
12	90,000	200	235	12,000	1,000	45	50	5	3	103
13	500,000	900	742	20,892	8,066	195	270	15	20	500
14	300,000	400	451	19,348	2,217	75	60	20	18	173
15	300,000	1,200	*a*432	*b*20,756	2,080	90	104	25	6	225
16	600,000	1,075	1,074	53,982	4,067	130	260	55	70	515
17	500,000	700	711	22,900	6,200	270	185	13	18	486
18	500,000	1,950	1,514	59,864	7,055	353	281	16	24	674
19	150,000	300	308	13,520	1,534	55	40	13	12	120
20	100,000	350	124	16,500	1,900	65	35	30	22	152
21	20,000	600	42	3,200	249	30	14	4	3	51
22	300,000	1,500	450	19,000	10,000	280	350	30	25	685
23	200,000	400	420	12,500	1,200	154	111	8	5	278

a Increased to 850 in 1898. *b* Increased to 35,800 in 1896.

COTTON CLOTHS—*Concluded.*

TABLE No. 1.—Capacity for Production—*Concluded.*

Number of Establishment.	Capital invested.	Horse power.	Looms in operation.	Spindles in operation.	Bales of cotton used in 1897.	Average number employed during 1897.				
						Men.	Women.	Boys.	Girls.	Total.
24	$10,000	99	15	1,400	250	10	4	.....	.....	14
25	2,500	25	24	....	*......	5	2	.....	1	8
26	1,000,000	800	754	19,976	2,879	348	169	17	13	547
27	200,000	75	150	8,200	636	30	36	4	.....	70
28	400,000	650	690	25,000	1,663	152	85	16	13	266
29	400,000	2,000	2,947	110,896	10,809	620	700	40	37	1,397
30	150,000	380	508	20,656	2,000	113	65	16	8	202
31	200,000	600	700	30,000	1,276	153	153	22	22	350
Total	$9,782,500	21,079	19,737	806,980	87,383	4,887	4,444	660	572	10,563

*Cotton yarns purchased.

COTTON WARPS, WEBS, THREADS AND YARNS.

TABLE No. 1.—Capacity for Production.

Number of Establishment.	Capital invested.	Horse power.	Looms in operation.	Spindles in operation.	Bales of cotton used in 1897.	Average number employed during 1897.				
						Men.	Women.	Boys.	Girls.	Total.
32	$1,000,000	750	550	15,000	3,000	215	496	50	75	836
33	50,000	150	....	3,000	420	33	28	2	2	65
34	20,000	100	....	980	400	8	2	1	1	12
35	300,000	500	....	17,000	1,325	80	56	16	20	172
36	40,000	90	....	4,500	500	19	13	3	5	40
37	40,000	80	....	3,200	439	20	12	.....	.....	32
38	30,000	100	....	1,500	1,584	20	.....	5	3	28
39	20,000	100	....	552	100	20	.....	.....	.....	20
40	30,000	30	....	600	250	4	4	.....	.....	8
41	40,000	50	....	3,500	477	31	13	5	1	50
42	175,000	200	....	2,912	535	26	30	3	3	62
43	125,000	40	100	....	*......	75	50	4	6	135
44	100,000	125	150	....	*......	25	275	.....	.....	300
45	50,000	85	43	....	*......	110	40	.....	.....	150
46	15,000	30	38	....	*......	12	13	.....	.....	25
47	50,000	40	35	....	*......	12	10	3	.....	25
48	75,000	100	140	....	*......	50	175	.....	.....	225
49	60,000	800	157	....	*......	175	75	.....	.....	250
50	594,200	900	....	39,000	1,360	100	200	25	25	350
51	50,000	20	....	3,000	*......	5	20	.....	.....	25
52	50,000	75	....	3,000	*......	10	18	2	3	33
53	60,000	130	....	5,000	500	40	50	10	.....	100
54	40,000	265	....	5,200	400	20	7	3	4	34

*Cotton yarns purchased.

COTTON WARPS, WEBS, THREADS AND YARNS—*Con'd.*

TABLE No. 1.—Capacity for Production—*Concluded.*

Number of Establishment.	Capital invested.	Horse Power.	Looms in operation.	Spindles in operation.	Bales of cotton used in 1897.	Average number employed during 1897.				
						Men.	Women.	Boys.	Girls.	Total.
55	$250,000	250	130	....	*......	75	75	.....	....	150
56	350,000	500	....	14,000	1,500	125	160	.....	.....	285
57	25,000	160	....	2,800	320	12	13	8	4	37
58	2,000,000	3,500	....	87,000	5,000	700	800	15	10	1,525
59	200,000	100	....	15,000	*160	19	46	1	.....	66
60	50,000	150	....	4,296	555	22	10	1	1	34
Total	$5,889,200	9,420	1,343	231,040	18,825	2,063	2,691	157	163	5,074

*Cotton yarns purchased.

ASSESSMENTS AND TAXES.

The commercial importance of the Textile industries to the State and to the towns can be no more clearly shown than by exhibiting in figures the amount assessed against the several establishments, for purposes of taxation, together with the amounts paid by them in taxes to the towns in which they are located. The following table shows the assessments and taxes paid by the thirty-one establishments represented in the table as engaged in the manufacture of cotton cloth.

COTTON CLOTHS.

Assessments and Taxes Paid, Divided by Towns.

Town.	Assessment on Grand List, 1897.	Amount paid in taxes, 1897.
Putnam	$742,700	$14,111.29
Plainfield	793,115	9,517.38
Brooklyn	542,142	5,692.50
Norwich	2,117,734	19,534.57
Killingly	544,807	8,171.10
Sprague	290,000	4,350.00
Mansfield	28,425	326.37
Montville	256,541	4,104.66
Windham	200,675	4,605.52
Huntington	140,000	2,100.00
Voluntown	75,000	1,350.00
New Hartford	326,040	3,912.48
Stonington	70,000	1,225.00
East Haddam	3,000	37.50
Canterbury	2,050	24.60
Griswold	645,000	6,450.00
Thompson	745,696	8,948.35
Total	$7,522,925	$94,461.32

ASSESSMENTS PER SPINDLE.

The same reference as in the foregoing can be made concerning the comparative assessments per spindle. It has been asserted that the methods of assessments of cotton mills in some States is made on a basis of spindles in use, and that Connecticut manufacturers suffer in comparison with these, by reason of the fact, which has been stated as being true, that the assessments made by the towns against Connecticut mills, when considered on the basis of spindle power, is excessive; how far or to what extent this contention can be borne out by the facts adduced, the following table will show. Certain it is, however, that the rate of assessment per spindle shows great irregularity in the systems of making assessments in the various towns.

It must be remembered in comparing the preceding with the table which follows, that while the total amount assessed is the same in each, yet the division by towns in the latter table show different amounts. This was rendered necessary by reason of the fact that some establishments were assessed in two or more towns, and therefore, in order to obtain accurately the rate of assessment per spindle, the total assessment should be used as a basis for the computation.

COTTON CLOTHS.

Assessment per Spindle by Towns.

Town.	Total assessment.	Number of spindles.	Rate of assessment per spindle.
Putnam	$742,700	81,544	$9.11
Plainfield	793,115	101,616	7.81
Norwich	*2,377,734	178,026	13.36
Killingly	*1,253,490	166,766	7.52
Thompson	745,696	110,896	6.72
Mansfield	28,425	10,704	2.66
Montville	†120,000	7,500	16.00
Windham	200,675	40,656	4.94
Canterbury	*2,050	....	....
Griswold	645,000	44,976	14.34
Huntington	140,000	11,696	11.97
Voluntown	75,000	16,500	4.55
New Hartford	326,040	22,300	14.69
Stonington	70,000	12,500	5.60
East Haddam	3,000	1,400	2.14
	$7,522,925	806,980	Average... $9.32
Less Canterbury (No spindles in use)	2,050		
Total	$7,520,875		

*Assessment in other towns added.
†Amount deducted for assessment in other towns.

COTTON WARPS, WEBS, THREADS AND YARNS.

Assessments and Taxes Paid, Divided by Towns.

Town.	Assessment on Grand List, 1897.	Amount paid in taxes, 1897.
Middletown	$352,910	$5,791.10
Middlefield	40,600	730.80
Haddam	39,000	663.00
Vernon	106,650	713.25
Plainfield	44,655	535.86
Griswold	93,850	938.50
Windham	1,194,070	27,453.61
East Haddam	104,152	1,301.40
Montville	10,000	160.00
Farmington	11,587	139.04
East Lyme	6,200	74.40
Bridgeport	78,000	936.00
Ansonia	38,000	836.00
Columbia	18,460	276.90
Norwalk	21,360	427.20
Waterbury	75,000	2,475.00
Hamden	64,950	974.25
Stonington	110,350	2,482.88
Westport	17,500	175.00
Killingly	14,190	212.85
Windsor Locks	112,150	1,121.50
Mansfield	24,795	371.92
Total	$2,578,429	$48,800.46

COTTON CLOTHS.

Table No. 2.—Capacity for Production.

Number of Establishment.	Pounds of cotton used during 1897.	Yards of goods produced during 1897.	Value of product manufactured.	Value per yard.	Per cent. production of full capacity.	Value of product, full capacity.
1	780,500	2,663,505	$99,000.00	3.7	95	$104,210.53
2	2,214,500	7,990,515	485,000.00	6.1	90	538,222.22
3	243,500	1,500,000	115,000.00	7.7	88	130,681.82
4	851,500	3,871,165	120,870.27	3.1	85	142,200.32
5	1,250,000	24,000,000	1,200,000.00	5.	100	1,200,000.00
6	450,000	1,650,000	75,865.86	4.6	95	79,858.80
7	1,727,000	3,920,700	291,180.11	7.4	100	291,180.11
8	711,500	2,556,580	128,791.61	5.	95	135,570.12
9	1,392,000	3,723,535	222,315.30	6.	94	236,505.64
10	905,500	2,976,000	116,641.44	3.9	87	134,070.28
11	625,000	5,124,641	168,809.32	3.3	95	177,694.02
12	500,000	3,000,000	70,000.00	2.3	75	93,333.33
13	4,033,000	10,081,608	604,895.00	6.	96	630,098.96
14	1,108,500	3,833,814	142,000.00	3.7	95	149,473.68
15	1,040,000	4,250,000	180,000.00	4.2	100	180,000.00
16	2,033,500	10,861,457	405,190.75	3.7	88	460,444.03
17	3,100,000	8,129,000	482,764.91	5.9	90	536,405.46
18	3,527,500	11,418,444	480,000.00	4.2	88	545,454.55
19	767,000	2,556,946	97,000.00	3.8	95	102,105.26
20	950,000	1,290,000	60,000.00	4.7	95	63,157.89
21	124,500	135,535	18,000.00	14.	67	26,865.67
22	5,000,000	4,221,410	522,034.09	12.3	100	522,034.09
23	600,000	4,000,000	307,000.00	7.7	100	307,000.00

COTTON CLOTHS—*Concluded.*

TABLE No. 2.—Capacity for Production—*Concluded.*

Number of Establishment.	Pounds of cotton used during 1897.	Yards of goods produced during 1897.	Value of product manufactured.	Value per yard.	Per cent. production of full capacity.	Value of product, full capacity.
24	125,000	107,210	$10,000.00	9.3	60	$16,666.67
25	*..........	133,380	9,000.00	6.7	50	18,000.00
26	1,439,500	5,070,106	391,355.72	7.7	80	489,194.65
27	*318,000	1,260,000	50,000.00	4.	80	60,250.00
28	831,500	2,827,060	189,960.79	6.7	82	231,659.50
29	5,404,500	19,323,087	1,040,000.00	5.4	100	1,040,000.00
30	1,000,000	3,537,496	126,934.08	3.6	100	126,934.08
31	638,000	6,054,779	278,055.26	4.6	100	278,055.26
Total	43,691,500	162,067,993	$8,487,664.51	5.2	†94	$9,047,326.94

*Cotton yarns purchased. †Average.

COTTON WARPS, WEBS, THREADS AND YARNS.

Table No. 2.—Capacity for Production.

Number of Establishment.	Pounds of cotton used during 1897.	Pounds of goods produced during 1897.	Yards of goods produced during 1897.	Dozens of goods produced during 1897.	Value of product manufactured.	Per cent. production of full capacity.	Value of product, full capacity.
32	*1,500,000	1,100,000	23,000,000	....	$852,000.00	100	$852,000.00
33	210,000	175,000	....	....	40,000.00	90	44,444.44
34	200,000	115,000	....	....	7,500.00	100	7,500.00
35	662,500	539,000	....	....	190,000.00	67	283,582.09
36	250,000	166,000	....	....	35,000.00	100	35,000.00
37	219,500	193,766	....	....	29,064.90	100	29,064.90
38	792,000	632,495	....	....	24,500.00	100	24,500.00
39	†50,000	†48,852	....	....	†80,000.00	90	88,888.89
40	125,000	100,000	....	....	10,000.00	33	30,303.03
41	238,500	180,793	....	....	39,505.01	50	79,010.02
42	267,500	218,277	....	....	35,800.00	60	59,666.67
43	‡.........	....	1,000,000	....	230,000.00	50	460,000.00
44	‡.........	....	4,000,000	....	400,000.00	100	400,000.00
45	‡.........	....	2,147,065	....	160,000.00	100	160,000.00
46	‡.........	....	....	286,532	28,000.00	100	28,000.00
47	‡.........	....	955,000	....	40,000.00	30	133,333.33
48	‡.........	....	4,294,120	....	300,000.00	75	400,000.00
49	‡.........	....	4,500,000	....	362,000.00	100	362,000.00
50	680,000	....	....	1,200,000	400,000.00	85	470,588.24
51	‡.........	112,000	....	....	75,000.00	75	100,000.00
52	‡.........	639,000	....	....	100,000.00	100	100,000.00
53	250,000	163,000	....	....	75,000.00	75	100,000.00
54	200,000	138,000	....	....	22,000.00	50	44,000.00

* 5,000 pounds other material used. † Other stock purchased and sold.
‡ Cotton yarns purchased.

COTTON WARPS, WEBS, THREADS AND YARNS—*Con'd.*

Table No. 2.—Capacity for Production—*Concluded.*

Number of Establishment.	Pounds of cotton used during 1897.	Pounds of goods produced during 1897.	Yards of goods produced during 1897.	Dozens of goods produced during 1897.	Value of product manufactured.	Per cent. production of full capacity.	Value of product, full capacity.
55	‡.........	....	2,250,000	....	$275,000.00	70	$392,857.14
56	750,000	637,500	....	....	320,000.00	80	400,000.00
57	160,000	116,000	....	....	27,500.00	100	27,500.00
58	2,500,000	2,000,000	....	....	2,700,000.00	90	3,000,000.00
59	‡80,000	....	....	1,100,000	165,000.00	70	235,714.29
60	277,500	212,268	....	....	30,000.00	95	31,589.47
Total	9,412,500	7,486,951	42,146,185	2,286,532	$7,052,869.91	84	$8,379,542.51

‡ Cotton yarns purchased.

COTTON CLOTHS, WARPS, WEBS, THREADS AND YARNS—Closed Mills.

Table No. 3.—Capacity for Production.

Number of Establishment.	Looms formerly in operation.	Spindles formerly in operation.
61	......	5,000
62	18	1,792
63	12	2,640
64	21	3,616
65	......	1,200
66	280	12,000
67	104	6,000
68	179	8,000
69	180	9,000
70	......	600
71	......	5,000
72	......	1,200
Total	794	56,048

COTTON CLOTHS, WARPS, WEBS, THREADS AND YARNS.

TABLE No. 4. — Assessments and Amounts Paid in Taxes — Division by Towns.

Town.	Assessment on Grand List, 1897.	Amount paid in taxes, 1897.
Ansonia	$38,000	$836.00
Bridgeport	78,000	936.00
Brooklyn	542,142	5,692.50
Bozrah	23,350	233.50
Canterbury	2,050	24.60
Colebrook	14,740	221.10
Columbia	18,460	276.90
Eastford	800	12.80
East Haddam	175,473	2,281.66
East Lyme	6,200	74.40
Farmington	11,587	139.04
Glastonbury	95,255	1,428.82
Griswold	738,850	7,388.50
Haddam	39,000	663.00
Hamden	64,950	974.25
Huntington	140,000	2,100.00
Killingly	578,557	8,677.35
Mansfield	53,220	698.29
Middlefield	40,600	730.80
Middletown	352,910	5,791.10
Montville	269,023	4,304.37
New Hartford	326,040	3,912.48
Norwalk	21,360	427.20

COTTON CLOTHS, WARPS, WEBS, THREADS AND YARNS — *Concluded.*

TABLE NO. 4. — Assessments and Amounts Paid in Taxes — Division by Towns — *Concluded.*

Town.	Assessment on Grand List, 1897.	Amount paid in taxes, 1897.
Norwich	$2,117,734	$19,534.57
Plainfield	837,770	10,053.24
Putnam	742,700	14,111.29
Sprague	290,000	4,350.00
Stonington	180,350	3,707.88
Thompson	745,696	8,948.35
Vernon	106,650	713.25
Voluntown	115,000	2,070.00
Waterbury	75,000	2,475.00
Westport	17,500	175.00
Windham	1,394,745	32,069.13
Windsor Locks	112,150	1,121.50
Woodstock	4,657	55.88
Total	$10,370,519	$147,209.75

COTTON — Closed Mills.

Assessments and Taxes Paid, Divided by Towns.

Town.	Assessment on Grand List, 1897.	Amount paid in taxes, 1897.
Glastonbury	$95,255	$1,428.82
East Haddam	68,821	942.76
Colebrook	14,740	221.10
Voluntown	40,000	720.00
Killingly	19,560	293.40
Bozrah	23,350	233.50
Eastford	800	12.80
Montville	2,482	39.71
Woodstock	4,657	55.88
Total	*$269,165	*$3,947.97

*Included in Table No. 4.

SYNOPSIS.

A synopsis of the foregoing shows that in the seventy-two establishments which appear in the tabulation, and which includes the mills which were closed during the period covered by the investigation, there were in 1897, 1,094,068 spindles, active and idle. The number of looms idle and in operation being 21,874. The total assessments against all the establishments represented, closed mills included, was $10,370,519, and the amount paid by them in taxes to the several towns $147,209.75, an average rate of $14\frac{2}{10}$ mills. The average rate of assessment in the entire State, computed on the basis of number of spindles, was $9.48 per spindle.

WAGE RATES AND RENT.

The table which follows shows the average wage rates which obtain in the sixty establishments which were in operation in 1897. A division in number of weavers and spinners, and information as to number of hours worked in the entire year by each individual not being obtainable, the actual average rate of wages cannot be shown. The accompanying table, however, contains an accurate statement as to the rates of wages for weavers and spinners which were paid in 1897 by each establishment.

The table also shows the number of tenements owned or controlled by the manufacturers represented, together with an approximate statement as to the number of rooms contained in each and the rate of monthly rental for each class. The total number of tenements reported as being occupied by employes in the cotton mills of the State was 3,084; the number of rooms contained in each ranging from 2 to 10, and the rate paid for rent from 90 cents to $11.00 per month.

COTTON CLOTHS, WARPS, WEBS, THREADS AND YARNS.

TABLE NO. 5.—Wage Rates and Rates Paid for Rent.

Number of Establishment.	WEAVERS. Weekly wage rates.			SPINNERS. Weekly wage rates.			Tenements owned.	Rooms in each.	Rent per month.
	Highest.	Lowest.	Average.	Highest.	Lowest.	Average.			
1	$12.00	$5.00	$7.00	$10.00	$8.50	$8.75	50	3 to 7	$2.00 to $4.17
2	13.22	3.00	6.27	11.92	7.00	9.15	248	3 to 8	1.86 to 3.73
3	8.50	5.00	7.00	9.00	6.00	8.00	52	4 to 7	2.25 to 4.00
4	7.50	3.50	5.75	9.80	6.00	7.90	52	3 to 7	2.24 to 4.56
5	10.50	6.25	7.50	14.00	10.25	12.00	450	3 to 7	2.50 to 5.00
6	7.00	5.90	6.50	8.00	8.00	8.00	32	3 to 6	3.38 to 4.17
7	10.50	6.00	7.00	10.00	6.00	8.50	......	....	....
8	9.10	4.56	6.82	9.00	8.60	8.72	39	3 to 7	3.50 to 7.00
9	12.00	6.60	7.00	10.50	9.00	9.50	110	4 to 8	2.43 to 5.42
10	8.88	4.39	6.17	8.48	7.25	8.23	57	4 to 6	3.25 to 6.50
11	11.80	5.40	7.80	6.24	2.55	4.65	......	....	....
12	7.50	5.00	6.00	10.50	5.50	7.00	25	3 to 6	2.00 to 4.00
13	8.82	4.00	6.25	6.18	3.00	4.75	73	3 to 7	3.00 to 5.42
14	12.00	5.00	7.00	10.00	8.50	8.75	48	5 to 7	4.00 to 5.00
15	8.50	6.00	7.78	9.00	7.50	8.34	56	4 to 7	3.43 to 5.25
16	8.00	5.00	6.00	9.00	7.00	7.50	160	4 to 7	2.80 to 3.20
17	9.49	4.06	6.66	7.00	8.50	5.00	123	3 to 7	3.60 to 7.00
18	10.97	3.10	6.56	11.33	8.92	9.70	175	3 to 9	1.82 to 5.20
19	12.00	5.00	7.00	10.00	8.50	8.75	59	3 to 7	2.00 to 4.17
20	9.00	4.80	6.00	5.50	2.56	4.00	50	3 to 8	2.00 to 4.00
21	7.50	4.00	5.00	5.10	3.00	4.60	40	5 to 10	1.50 to 6.25
22	8.00	4.50	5.50	5.50	3.50	5.00	150	2 to 10	.90 to 9.00
23	11.52	5.01	8.10	10.59	3.00	4.94	55	6	6.00

COTTON CLOTHS, WARPS, WEBS, THREADS AND YARNS—*Continued.*

TABLE No. 5.—Wage Rates and Rates Paid for Rent—*Continued.*

Number of Establishment.	Weavers. Weekly wage rates.			Spinners. Weekly wage rates.			Tenements owned.	Rooms in each.	Rent per month.
	Highest.	Lowest.	Average.	Highest.	Lowest.	Average.			
24	$7.50	$6.00	$7.00	$6.00	$5.00	$5.75	7	6 to 8	$3.50 to $4.00
25	9.00	6.50	7.25	7.00	6.00	6.75	12	5	5.00
26	10.25	4.00	6.00	6.30	1.80	4.16	150	3 to 8	3.25 to 8.66
27	7.00	5.00	6.00	8.00	6.00	7.25	31	5 to 7	2.50 to 3.75
28	12.00	4.00	7.00	5.64	1.92	4.00	80	3 to 8	2.70 to 8.00
29	......	......	......	......	......	......	......	....	....
30	10.50	7.50	9.50	6.00	4.50	5.00	54	3 to 7	3.00 to 5.12
31	10.50	4.50	8.00	14.00	9.00	11.00	68	3 to 5	2.00 to 6.00
32	15.00	6.00	9.00	8.40	5.50	6.00	72	7	6.00
33	......	......	......	8.25	6.00	7.00	12	4 to 7	3.00 to 6.00
34	......	......	......	9.00	6.00	7.25	4	5	3.50
35	......	......	......	6.30	4.50	5.40	62	3 to 7	2.20 to 5.00
36	......	......	......	10.00	7.00	8.50	13	3 to 6	3.00 to 6.25
37	......	......	......	5.00	4.50	4.87	13	6 to 10	4.00 to 7.00
38	......	......	......	6.50	4.00	5.00	16	5 to 7	4.00 to 6.00
39	......	......	......	10.00	8.00	9.00	......	....	....
40	......	......	......	5.00	4.00	4.25	6	6 to 10	2.50 to 4.50
41	......	......	......	6.00	4.80	5.40	......	....	....
42	......	......	......	7.00	4.00	5.00	18	4 to 10	2.00 to 6.25
43	30.00	8.00	18.00	......	......	......	......	....	....
44	14.00	5.00	7.00	......	......	......	......	....	....
45	21.00	9.00	15.00	......	......	......	......	....	....
46	6.00	2.00	5.40	6.00	2.00	5.40	14	2 to 6	1.25 to 4.00

COTTON CLOTHS, WARPS, WEBS, THREADS AND YARNS—*Concluded.*

TABLE No. 5.—Wage Rates and Rates Paid for Rent—*Concluded.*

Number of Establishment.	WEAVERS. Weekly wage rates.			SPINNERS. Weekly wage rates.			Tenements owned.	Rooms in each.	Rent per month.
	Highest.	Lowest.	Average.	Highest.	Lowest.	Average.			
47	$21.00	$5.00	$14.00	......	......	......	......	......	....
48	12.00	6.00	8.00	......	......	......	......	......	....
49	12.00	8.00	9.00	......	......	......	22	6 to 9	$8.00 to $10.00
50	......	......	......	$14.50	$6.00	$9.00	30	6 to 8	7.00 to 11.00
51	......	......	......	6.00	4.80	5.60	......	......	....
52	......	......	......	8.00	4.00	5.00	......	......	....
53	......	......	......	8.00	4.00	4.50	32	5 to 6	3.00 to 5.00
54	......	......	......	8.00	1.80	4.50	23	4 to 7	1.60 to 4.00
55	......	......	......	14.00	6.00	9.00	6	4 to 9	4.00 to 10.00
56	......	......	......	9.00	5.00	6.50	12	4	4.17
57	......	......	......	8.00	6.00	6.75	20	4 to 6	2.50 to 4.00
58	......	......	......	13.00	5.50	6.97	178	3 to 8	2.50 to 10.00
59	......	......	......	12.00	5.75	7.25	7	6 to 8	5.00 to 7.00
60	......	......	......	8.00	6.50	7.00	18	4 to 6	2.75 to 4.00

ILLUSTRATIONS.

The following exhibits are taken from the completed schedules of different manufacturers of all grades of cotton goods, the purpose being to show the number of spindles per employe, the number of yards produced per loom, and the per cent. of product value paid in wages by establishments.

As has been before stated, much of the information secured by the Bureau for publication in this chapter of the report was obtained with the understanding that the identity of the establishment furnishing the data was not to be disclosed. The twelve schedules presented herewith, however, while giving the amount paid in wages, together with the value of product, separately, do not in any degree violate the agreement made as to concealment of the identity of the establishments with which such agreement had been entered into.

EXHIBIT 1.

Year 1897.
307 looms, 14,640 spindles,
Produced 2,663,505 yards sheetings, shirtings and twills.
Average number employed, 126.
Number spindles per employe, 116.19.
Average yards produced per loom, 8,676.
Value of product, $99,000.00.
Amount paid in wages, $43,000.00.
Per cent. of product value paid in wages, 43.4.

EXHIBIT 2.

Year 1897.
282 looms, 15,296 spindles,
Produced 1,500,000 yards cotton cloth.
Average number employed, 157.
Number spindles per employe, 97.43.
Average yards produced per loom, 5,319.
Value of product, $115,000.00.
Amount paid in wages, $38,475.97.
Per cent. of product value paid in wages, 33.5.

EXHIBIT 3.

Year 1897.
451 looms, 21,080 spindles,
Produced 3,871,165 yards sheetings.
Average number employed, 190.
Number spindles per employe, 110.95.
Average yards produced per loom, 8,584.
Value of product, $120,870.27.
Amount paid in wages, $47,527.36.
Per cent. of product value paid in wages, 39.3.

EXHIBIT 4.

Year 1897.
2,775 looms, 118,938 spindles,
Produced 24,000,000 yards cotton cloth.
Average number employed, 1,500.
Number spindles per employe, 79.29.
Average yards produced per loom, 8,649.
Value of product, $1,200,000.00.
Amount paid in wages, $500,000.00.
Per cent. of product value paid in wages, 41.7.

EXHIBIT 5.

Year 1897.
172 looms, 10,704 spindles,
Produced 1,650,000 yards sheetings and twills.
Average number employed, 99.
Number spindles per employe, 108.12.
Average yards produced per loom, 9,218.
Value of product, $75,865.86.
Amount paid in wages, $26,317.04.
Per cent. of product value paid in wages, 34.7.

EXHIBIT 6.

Year 1897.
300 looms, 13,280 spindles,
Produced 2,556,580 yards sheetings.
Average number employed, 142.
Number spindles per employe, 93.52.
Average yards produced per loom, 8,522.
Value of product, $128,791.61.
Amount paid in wages, $41,909.17.
Per cent. of product value paid in wages, 32.5.

EXHIBIT 7.

Year 1897.
648 looms, 23,640 spindles,
Produced 3,723,535 yards sheetings.
Average number employed, 274.
Number spindles per employe, 84.73.
Average yards produced per loom, 5,746.
Value of product, $222,315.30.
Amount paid in wages, $77,671.53.
Per cent. of product value paid in wages, 34.9.

EXHIBIT 8.

Year 1897.
451 looms, 19,348 spindles,
Produced 3,833.814 yards sheetings, shirtings and twills.
Average number employed, 173.
Number spindles per employe, 111.84.
Average yards produced per loom, 8,501.
Value of product, $142,000.00.
Amount paid in wages, $55,000.00.
Per cent. of product value paid in wages, 38.7.

EXHIBIT 9.

Year 1897.
308 looms, 13,520 spindles,
Produced 2,556,946 yards sheetings, shirtings and twills.
Average number employed, 120.
Number spindles per employe, 112.67.
Average yards produced per loom, 8,302.
Value of product, $97,000.00.
Amount paid in wages, $42,000.00.
Per cent. of product value paid in wages, 43.3.

EXHIBIT 10.

Year 1897.
690 looms, 25,000 spindles,
Produced 2,827,080 yards cambrics, satines and twills.
Average number employed, 266.
Number spindles per employe, 93.98.
Average yards produced per loom, 4,097.
Value of product, $189,960.79.
Amount paid in wages, $82,641.87.
Per cent. of product value paid in wages, 43.5.

EXHIBIT 11.

Year 1897.
508 looms, 20,656 spindles,
Produced 3,537,496 yards sheetings and twills.
Average number employed, 202.
Number spindles per employe, 102.26.
Average yards produced per loom, 6,967.
Value of product, $126,934.08.
Amount paid in wages, $50,000.00.
Per cent. of product value paid in wages, 39.4.

EXHIBIT 12.

Year 1897.
700 looms, 30,000 spindles,
Produced 6,054,779 yards fine yarn goods.
Average number employed, 350.
Number spindles per employe, 85.71.
Average yards produced per loom, 8,650.
Value of product, $278,055.26.
Amount paid in wages, $104,325.79.
Per cent. of product value paid in wages, 37.5.

COMPARATIVE CONDITIONS.

Manufacturers and employes engaged in the cotton industry in Connecticut have been mutually interested in the extension of cotton manufacturing in the South, and its effect upon the industry in Connecticut. In New England nearly uniform laws respecting hours of labor and employment of children make the conditions more equal in the competition of these States. In the large cotton centers of Massachusetts and Maine a reduction has been made in wages, the manufacturers claiming that it was necessary to enable them to make goods in competition with the low wages and long hours in the South. The cotton industry, occupying as it does such a prominent place in Connecticut, comparisons with former conditions are of interest.

In the United States Census of 1890, Connecticut ranks fourth in the number of cotton spindles, having 934,155, or 5.6 per cent. of the entire number, being exceeded, respectively, by Massachusetts, Rhode Island and New Hampshire, in the order named.

From the same source the figures show that there were employed in the cotton industry 13,411 persons with a yearly pay-roll aggregating $4,524,483. The value of the product is given as $15,409,476. It has been said that, while the prestige long held by New England as the cotton manufacturing stronghold was fast departing on account of the gigantic advance and competition in the South, Connecticut was not holding its own in the strife. A study of the following table, compiled from Dockham's Textile Directory for a period of ten years, 1887–1896, the accuracy of which is to be assumed, shows the assertion to be true.

NUMBER OF COTTON SPINDLES.

	1887.	1889.	1891.	1892.	1894.	1896.	Percentages of increase + or decrease — in 1896 as compared with 1887.
NEW ENGLAND STATES.							
CONNECTICUT....	1,092,524	1,023,928	1,046,399	1,020,070	1,033,935	1,045,937	—4.26
Maine..............	824,432	884,722	917,169	923,541	931,116	916,304	+11.14
New Hampshire....	1,180,648	1,207,312	1,245,021	1,288,351	1,296,606	1,308,802	+10.85
Vermont............	63,868	62,775	72,848	80,271	102,303	106,583	+66.88
Massachusetts.......	5,330,120	5,905,875	6,308,925	6,847,744	7,160,480	7,790,642	+46.16
Rhode Island.......	1,856,982	1,948,958	2,036,519	2,086,087	2,076,665	2,104,060	+13.31
SOUTHERN STATES.							
Alabama............	104,791	96,647	102,519	138,471	170,159	231,011	+120.45
Georgia..............	406,330	442,148	484,963	501,512	550,510	731,238	+79.96
Kentucky...........	27,500	42,500	47,287	49,143	50,043	58,779	+113.74
Mississippi..........	47,050	54,800	57,420	57,968	54,484	72,258	+53.58
North Carolina.....	227,348	321,070	423,192	510,190	656,480	910,474	+300.48
South Carolina......	232,692	351,040	463,424	508,404	626,883	997,185	+328.54
Tennessee...........	100,277	116,783	124,911	117,841	121,984	145,428	+45.03
Virginia.............	68,912	79,612	91,760	111,756	139,356	134,696	+95.46

THE INDUSTRY IN CONNECTICUT AND IN THE SOUTH—1890.

The data available for comparison respecting the conditions in Connecticut and in those Southern States in which the manufacture of cotton goods has had its greatest increase are to be found in the United States Census, and being brought up to 1890 only, can only form the basis of broad, general inferences as to product, wages, employes, etc.

The following table summarizes this information, and presents certain percentages so as to show the facts clearly from the latest returns, namely, those for the year 1890.

COTTON INDUSTRY IN CONNECTICUT AND THE SOUTH—1890.

States.	Value of goods made.	Value of stock used.	Value of industry product.	Amount of wages paid.	Profit and minor expense fund.	Percentages of industry product paid in wages.	Percentages of industry product devoted to profit and minor expenses.
CONNECTICUT	$15,409,476	$8,208,111	$7,201,365	$4,239,546	$2,961,819	58.95	41.05
Alabama........	2,190,771	1,459,048	731,723	402,908	328,815	55.06	44.94
Georgia.........	12,035,629	7,778,026	4,257,603	2,167,036	2,090,567	50.90	49.10
Kentucky.......	1,000,668	643,949	356,719	170,573	186,146	47.82	52.18
Mississippi......	1,333,398	871,970	461,428	263,997	196,431	57.21	42.79
North Carolina.	9,563,443	6,238,352	3,325,091	1,475,932	1,849,159	44.39	55.61
South Carolina..	9,800,798	6,816,820	2,983,978	1,510,494	1,473,484	50.62	49.38
Tennessee.......	2,507,719	1,765,062	742,657	444,573	298,084	59.86	40.14
Virginia.......	1,732,648	1,197,234	535,414	373,993	161,421	69.85	30.15

It will be seen from the foregoing figures that the value of cotton goods made in Connecticut in 1890 amounted to $15,409,476, exceeding the product of any of the Southern group, Georgia leading with $12,035,629, South Carolina standing next with a product of $9,800,798, and North Carolina next with a product of $9,563,443.

The value of the stock used in Connecticut, including under that term not only all that may be called raw material, but also all the incidental items of stock or material which enter into the product or which are consumed in the process of manufacture, was $8,208,111. In Georgia the value of stock used was $7,778,026; in South Carolina $6,816,820, and in North Carolina $6,238,352. By deducting the value of stock used and material consumed, as shown by these figures, from the value of goods made, there remains what may be termed the "industry product," or the value product actually created in the cotton industry. By this method it is found that the value of the industry product in Connecticut was $7,201,365; in Georgia $4,257,603; in South Carolina $2,983,978, and in North Carolina $3,325,091.

This industry product may be divided into two parts, one being the aggregate sum paid in wages, and the other constituting a fund from which all the minor expenses of manufacture, such as taxes, insurance, interest, etc., must be paid, and from which, after these minor expenses have been provided for, profits are derived. It follows that as the portion of industry product devoted to wages is increased or diminished, the balance devoted to profit and minor expenses will be diminished or increased.

In order to note the relative proportions in each of the States it is only needed to refer to the percentages of industry product paid in wages, and of industry product devoted to profit and minor expenses, as shown in the last two columns of the table. It is there shown that in the year under consideration 58.95 per cent. of the industry product in Connecticut was divided among the operatives in the form of wages, leaving a balance of 41.05 per cent. to be devoted to profits and the minor expenses of manufacture, expenses, which it should be borne in mind, are only termed "minor" in comparison with the greater expense of wages and stock used, inasmuch as in themselves they may constitute a considerable percentage of expense.

It will be noted that there are two States in the Southern group in which the percentage paid in wages is higher than in Connecticut. These are Tennessee and Virginia, but the product is comparatively small.

The Commissioner of the Massachusetts Bureau of Labor Statistics, in a report on this same subject, says, "It is probable that the establishments were not so effectively organized as the others."

As against the 41.05 per cent. devoted to profits and minor expenses in Connecticut, there remained in Georgia 49.10, in South Carolina 49.38 per cent., and in North Carolina 55.61 per cent. Of course these percentages show nothing conclusively as to profits, since the element of minor expense is not determinable from the figures and may be greater or less than in Connecticut. If less, then on the basis of these figures, a larger share of the industry product could be devoted to profits in these States than in Connecticut. If greater, it might still be possible to secure the same profits as in Connecticut, unless they were so great as to overcome the larger proportion which, in the aggregate, appears as a profit and minor expense fund.

COMPARATIVE FIGURES FOR 1880.

For the purpose of showing historically the growth of the cotton industry in Connecticut and the Southern States, during the ten years preceding 1890, the following table is introduced, derived from the Census of 1880.

States.	Value of goods made.	Value of stock used.	Value of industry product.	Amount of wages paid.	Profit and minor expense fund.	Percentages of industry product paid in wages.	Percentages of industry product devoted to profit and minor expenses.
CONNECTICUT	$16,069,771	$8,029,127	$8,040,644	$3,632,639	$4,408,005	45.18	54.82
Alabama........	1,228,019	783,711	444,308	239,998	204,310	54.02	45.98
Georgia.........	6,481,894	4,019,673	2,462,221	1,135,184	1,327,037	46.10	53.90
Kentucky.......	418,286	253,818	164,468	63,850	100,618	38.82	61.18
Mississippi......	679,093	337,149	341,944	133,214	208,730	38.96	61.04
North Carolina.	2,554,482	1,463,645	1,090,837	439,659	651,178	40.30	59.70
South Carolina..	2,895,769	1,808,300	1,087,469	380,844	706,625	35.02	64.98
Tennessee.......	874,717	553,761	320,956	161,071	159,885	50.18	49.82
Virginia........	1,040,962	640,391	400,571	169,789	230,782	42.39	57.61

In this year it will be seen that the total value of goods made in Connecticut was $16,069,771, or 4.11 per cent. less than in 1890. This may properly be accounted for by the cheaper cost of material, thus lessening the selling price of the product.

During this period Georgia practically doubled her product, and North and South Carolina both show a gain of more than 235 per cent.

Without considering the other figures in the table, it is interesting to note the percentages of industry product paid in wages and devoted to profit and minor expenses in the leading States in 1880, as compared with those before cited for 1890. As to the percentage of industry product paid in wages, Connecticut, in 1890, shows 45.18, as against 58.95 in 1890, a considerable increase in the latter year. Georgia shows a slight increase, namely, from 46.10 per cent. to 50.90 per cent. South Carolina rose from 35.02 to 50.62, and North Carolina from 40.30 to 44.39. It is seen that in each of these States wages consumed a larger portion of the industry product in 1890 than in 1880, but the gain was greater in Connecticut than in any of the other States, except Mississippi, South Carolina and Virginia.

The table further shows that while in 1880 54.82 per cent. of the industry product was devoted to profit and minor expenses, this percentage fell to 41.05 per cent. in 1890, while on the other hand, the percentage in Georgia fell only from 53.90 to 49.10, and in North Carolina from 59.70 to 55.61. In South Carolina the decline was from 64.98 per cent. to 49.38 per cent.

PERCENTAGES OF STOCK AND WAGES OF PRODUCT, 1880-1890.

The table that follows shows the percentages of the value of stock used and wages paid of the value of goods made—that is, of the selling price of the product in 1880.

PERCENTAGES OF STOCK AND WAGES OF PRODUCT.

States.	Stock used of product.	Wages paid of product.
CONNECTICUT	48.68	22.61
Alabama	63.82	19.54
Georgia	62.01	17.51
Kentucky	60.68	15.26
Mississippi	49.65	.19.62
North Carolina	57.30	17.21
South Carolina	62.45	13.15
Tennessee	63.31	18.41
Virginia	61.52	16.31

In Connecticut the value of stock consumed represented 48.68 per cent. of the selling price of the product, while wages represented 22.61 per cent. In Georgia stock represented 62.01 per cent. and wages 17.51 per cent. In North Carolina stock 57.30 per cent. and wages 17.21 per cent. In South Carolina stock 62.45 per cent. and wages 13.15 per cent.

To put it another way, out of every $100 received for the product, $48.68 was expended for stock and $22.61 for wages in Connecticut, and $57.30 for stock and $19.62 for wages in North Carolina.

It will be noticed that in Connecticut the percentage paid in wages was larger than any of the other States. For purpose of comparison the same figures for 1890 are arranged in the table that follows:

States.	Stock used of product.	Wages paid of product.
CONNECTICUT	53.27	27.51
Alabama	66.60	18.39
Georgia	64.63	18.01
Kentucky	64.35	17.05
Mississippi	65.39	19.80
North Carolina	65.23	15.43
South Carolina	69.55	15.41
Tennessee	70.39	17.73
Virginia	69.10	21.59

From this table it appears that in 1890 the value of the stock consumed in Connecticut was 53.27 per cent. of the selling price of the product, and wages 27.51 per cent. The percentage of wages paid of selling price is, as in 1880, larger in Connecticut than in any of the Southern States, and very much larger than in North and South Carolina, which show percentages of 15.41 and 15.43, respectively. Georgia shows a percentage of 18.01.

The difference between the amount of wages paid, considered as a percentage of the selling price of the product in Connecticut as compared with North and South Carolina and Georgia, is still wider in 1890 than in 1880, and greatly so in North Carolina.

In 1890 the difference between North and South Carolina is small as compared with 1880.

COMPARISON OF AVERAGE WEEKLY EARNINGS.
1890.

States.	Operatives and skilled employes.			Unskilled employes.
	Males above 16 years.	Females above 15 years.	Children.	Males above 16 years.
CONNECTICUT	$7.68	$5.69	$3.35	$7.92
Alabama	5.31	4.19	1.78	4.77
Georgia	5.75	4.55	1.96	6.09
Kentucky	5.89	4.02	1.89	5.40
Mississippi	7.09	4.66	1.67	7.09
North Carolina	5.25	3.21	1.84	4.71
South Carolina	5.17	3.90	1.93	5.00
Tennessee	6.31	3.24	2.30	6.10
Virginia	6.29	3.54	2.11	6.30

In this table the operatives and skilled employes are classified separately from the unskilled employes, and each class is subdivided into groups of males above 16 years of age, females above 15 years of age, and children.

It will be seen that the wages of the skilled employes in Connecticut, $7.68, $5.69 and $3.35 for the respective grades, is greater than in any of the Southern group. The lowest being males above 16 years, in Georgia, $5.75. For females above 15 years, in North Carolina, $3.21, and for children, in Mississippi, $1.67. No quotation is given for Connecticut for females and children in the unskilled class. That given for males above 16 years is $7.92. The lowest is in North Carolina, $4.71. It will be noted, however, that notwithstanding these apparent differences in nominal wages, the labor cost appears to be more nearly equalized when put upon the basis of cost per spindle, as shown in the following table.

It is not pretended that the conditions that existed in 1890 exist to-day. In but two States are the figures collected annually under statute law (Massachusetts and North Carolina). The last report of the North Carolina Bureau of Labor Statistics, covering the year 1897, has interesting data which may be compared with similar data collected by this Bureau, covering the same period.

COMPARISONS RELATING TO COST OF MANUFACTURE SHOWN BY THE CENSUS OF 1890.

The tables that follow are for the purpose of showing a comparison of different elements entering into the cost of manufacture in each of the States considered.

The first shows the average cost per pound of cotton, percentages of children of total wage-earners, number of spindles per employe, labor cost per spindle and cost of fuel, on basis of spindles, derived from the Census of 1890.

COMPARISONS RELATING TO COST OF MANUFACTURE SHOWN BY 1890 CENSUS.

States.	Average cost per pound of cotton.	Per cent. of children of total wage-earners.	Number of spindles per employe.	Labor cost per spindle.	Cost of fuel on basis of spindles.
CONNECTICUT	$.1076	7.90	70.66	$4.54	$.[illegible]
Alabama	.0932	23.99	37.95	5.09	0.30
Georgia	.0964	23.85	43.19	4.86	0.32
Kentucky	.0964	21.76	52.50	3.97	0.20
Mississippi	.0939	26.52	49.40	4.63	0.49
North Carolina	.1008	24.32	39.67	4.37	0.30
South Carolina	.0975	26.52	41.23	4.54	0.33
Tennessee	.0985	20.20	45.92	4.56	0.49
Virginia	.1018	23.92	47.38	3.97	0.18

It appears from the table that the average cost per pound of the cotton used in Connecticut was .1076. This is higher than in any of the other States, but only slightly higher than in Virginia.

When the percentages of children of total wage-earners is considered, a very different condition appears in Connecticut than in the other States. The percentage in Connecticut is 7.90; in South Carolina it is 26.52; in North Carolina 24.32, and in Georgia 23.85.

In number of spindles per employe, Connecticut shows 70.66, while North Carolina returned but 39.67, South Carolina 41.23, and Georgia 43.19.

In a comparison of the labor cost per spindle per employe, in Connecticut, the figures are $4,54, while it is $4.37 in North Carolina, $4.54 in South Carolina, and $4.86 in Georgia. How much conditions have changed since these figures were collected it is impossible to say. Correspondence was had with officials of the Southern States to ascertain, if possible, what the present conditions are, but without success.

*"A general decline in the net price of cotton, unaccompanied by a relative change in freight and other charges which finally determine its price at the mill, would probably bear equally upon all the States, and would simply change the amounts of the figures without changing their returns."

It is probable, however, that the proportion of children of total wage-earners has been changed, as the age at which children may be employed has been raised from thirteen years, as it was at the time these figures were collected, to fourteen years at the present time.

The cost of fuel, on the basis of spindles, was but 22 cents in Connecticut, while it was 33 cents in South Carolina, 32 cents in Georgia, and 30 cents in North Carolina.

In connection with the cost of fuel, the table that follows shows this cost computed as a percentage of the value of the product (this being the fairest basis of comparison), and includes other data relating to fuel and motive power.

---

*Mass. Report.

COMPARISONS RELATING TO COST OF MANUFACTURE, CENSUS 1890.

States.	Relative proportions of cost of fuel.			Percentages of motive power.		Percentages of cost of fuel of value of product.
	Coal.	Wood.	Other fuel.	Steam.	Water.	
CONNECTICUT.	87.12	0.50	12.38	35.13	64.87	1.31
Alabama	82.69	17.31	....	58.20	41.80	1.09
Georgia	89.17	10.19	0.64	35.43	64.57	1.17
Kentucky........	86.21	13.79	....	95.29	4.71	0.87
Mississippi........	58.05	41.95	....	98.18	1.82	2.11
North Carolina..	44.57	51.38	4.05	47.57	52.43	1.05
South Carolina..	83.45	13.60	2.95	42.38	57.62	1.13
Tennessee........	88.84	11.16	....	81.08	18.92	1.90
Virginia..........	97.67	2.33	....	17.87	82.13	0.99

This table presents the relative proportions of coal and wood used in the different States considered, the relative proportions of steam and water power of the entire motive power in the industry, and the percentages which the cost of fuel constitutes of value of product.

In Connecticut coal represented 87.12 per cent. of the entire fuel consumed, other fuel 12.38 per cent., and wood only .50.

In Georgia coal represented 89.17 per cent. and wood 10.19 per cent. In South Carolina coal represented 83.45 per cent. and wood 13.60 per cent., but in North Carolina coal represented only 44.57 per cent., and the percentage of wood rose to 51.38.

In Connecticut 64.87 per cent. of the motive power was derived from water, and only 35.13 from steam.

In Georgia steam represented 35.43 per cent. and water 64.57 per cent. In North Carolina steam represented 47.57 per cent. and water 52.43 per cent., and in South Carolina the percentage of steam was 42.38 per cent. and water 57.62 per cent.

In Connecticut the expense of fuel amounted to 1.31 per cent. of the value of the product.

In Georgia 1.17 per cent.; in North Carolina 1.05 per cent., and in South Carolina 1.13 per cent.

Notwithstanding the differences in certain elements of manufacture, by combining the value of stock and materials consumed and the amount of wages paid, and computing them as a percentage of the total value of product, it is found that there is a very slight difference between the States.

In some instances this percentage is higher in the Southern States than in Connecticut. The figures are brought together in the table that follows.

PERCENTAGES OF STOCK AND WAGES OF VALUE OF PRODUCT.

CONNECTICUT	80.78
Alabama	84.99
Georgia	82.64
Kentucky	81.40
Mississippi	85.19
North Carolina	80.66
South Carolina	84.96
Tennessee	88.12
Virginia	90.69

In Connecticut the combined value of stock and wages represented 80.78 per cent. of the selling price of the product. In Georgia it was 82.64 per cent., South Carolina 84.96 per cent., and in North Carolina 80.66 per cent., the smallest of any of the Southern States.

WOOLEN.

The following tables refer to those establishments in the State which were engaged in the manufacture of goods composed wholly or in part of wool. The computation as to quantity of material used is based on the amount of "scoured wool" used, to which, it must be stated, the amount of "other material used" should be added. This "other material" consists of "woolen rags," "shoddy," "mixed stock" and "cotton."

It is found, therefore, that the quantity of wool used in the fifty-four establishments represented in the tabulation amounted to 17,626,388 pounds during the year 1897, to which amount should be added 4,041,171 pounds of "other material."

As to amount of capital invested, it should be borne in mind that the total amount as shown in the tables, refers to "capital originally invested," or "capital stock of corporation," which, obviously, is not intended to include accumulations or surplus. The amount thus given as being invested in the woolen industries of Connecticut in 1897 was $6,906,000.00. There were 417 sets of cards in use, 3,213 looms, and 91,928 spindles in operation during the year. The total average number employed in all establishments was 7,738, of which 4,761 were men, 2,507 women, and 470 boys and girls under 16 years of age. The proportion of boys and girls of total number employed was 6.1 per cent.

WOOLEN.

TABLE No. 1.—Capacity for Production.

Number of Establishment.	Capital invested.	Horse power.	Sets of cards.	Looms in operation.	Spindles in operation.	Pounds of wool used in 1897.	Average number employed during 1897.				
							Men.	Women.	Boys.	Girls.	Total.
1	$10,000	150	2	36	1,244	[1] 27,531	33	19	4	2	58
2	35,000	50	2	21	792	[2] 40,000	36	10	4	2	52
3	18,000	75	2	14	792	125,000	40	4	2	....	46
4	300,000	300	19	88	......	405,000	129	63	5	....	197
5	50,000	200	5	22	1,480	275,000	53	19	5	2	79
6	24,000	125	7	38	2,140	200,000	60	30	....	....	90
7	240 000	270	9	109	......	[3] 308,556	200	88	15	8	311
8	200,000	350	.....	50	3,732	300,000	25	25	20	20	90
9	25,000	80	4	20	1,680	[4] 90,000	35	9	....	....	44
10	100,000	125	12	58	3,784	378,662	90	53	....	3	146
11	100,000	250	15	76	......	123,400	192	60	....	....	252
12	200,000	150	......	63	......	[3] 840,000	35	100	....	25	160
13	25,000	80	3	28	816	[5] 17,000	31	17	....	....	48
14	32,000	100	4	25	936	240,000	37	20	3	....	60
15	200,000	300	20	125	......	273,228	209	78	7	5	299
16	300,000	300	9	160	3,500	288,500	264	95	8	8	375
17	160,000	200	10	54	3,690	312,000	71	41	2	....	114
18	250,000	500	5	114	......	275,000	216	64	8	15	303
19	75,000	120	4	19	1,800	[6] 100,000	70	15	2	....	87
20	10,000	160	1	24	288	[7] 55,000	20	6	....	....	26
21	250,000	400	20	67	6,000	627,451	100	70	2	3	175
22	75,000	150	5	70	1,584	[8] 300,000	60	35	....	....	95
23	100,000	200	7	46	......	325,000	84	23	3	4	114

[1] 22,100 pounds other material used.
[2] 45,000 " " " "
[3] Including worsted yarns purchased.
[4] 15,000 pounds other material used.
[5] 27,500 " " " "
[6] 125,000 " " " "
[7] 100,000 " " " "
[8] 500,000 " " " "

WOOLEN — *Continued.*

Table No. 1. — Capacity for Production — *Continued.*

Number of Establishment.	Capital invested.	Horse power.	Sets of cards.	Looms in operation.	Spindles in operation.	Pounds of wool used in 1897.	Average number employed during 1897.				
							Men.	Women.	Boys.	Girls.	Total.
24	$10,000	160	6	43	......	[9] 150,000	50	25	5	....	80
25	25,000	40	4	27	600	[10] 180,448	32	21	....	....	53
26	200,000	180	14	......	......	[11] 491,946	60	10	....	....	70
27	75,000	150	8	36	2,800	500,000	70	50	....	....	120
28	100,000	225	7	40	2,150	[12] 221,053	78	25	3	1	107
29	45,000	116	5	35	1,680	371,200	65	35	....	....	100
30	50,000	180	7	35	2,688	[13] 558,568	75	28	....	....	103
31	100,000	350	16	118	3,080	1,200,000	215	75	....	7	297
32	20,000	75	3	16	1,040	132,000	26	6	2	....	34
33	150,000	300	3	17	864	[14] 475,000	60	20	4	....	84
34	15,000	60	4	42	960	[15] 25,000	24	14	3	....	41
35	40,000	65	4	28	2,080	80,000	23	13	4	3	43
36	15,000	75	4	17	1,320	40,000	40	10	3	2	55
37	15,000	85	5	27	1,968	[16] 65,000	61	9	4	4	78
38	[illegible]	1,200	25	424	13,444	2,700,000	412	423	32	36	903
39	75,000	150	10	88	......	430,000	100	50	....	....	150
40	50,000	125	6	35	2,800	300,000	80	20	....	....	100
41	200,000	125	6	60	1,520	120,000	64	30	3	3	100
42	25,000	75	3	14	800	60,000	28	8	....	....	36
43	400,000	300	17	100	5,600	595,845	175	80	20	25	300
44	150,000	200	14	70	......	328,000	80	60	3	2	145
45	7,000	60	......	......	1,200	21,000	12	......	....	....	12
46	65,000	70	3	32	......	[17] 7,000	34	16	4	....	54

[9] 300,000 pounds other material used.
[10] 14,381 " " " "
[11] 47,474 " " " "
[12] 25,500 " " " "
[13] 13,500 " " " "
[14] 35,000 " " " "
[15] 100,000 " " "
[16] 128,216 " " "
[17] 295,000 " " "

WOOLEN — *Concluded.*

Table No. 1. — Capacity for Production — *Concluded.*

Number of Establishment.	Capital invested.	Horse power.	Sets of cards.	Looms in operation.	Spindles in operation.	Pounds of wool used in 1897.	Average number employed during 1897. Men.	Women.	Boys.	Girls.	Total.
47	$60,000	150	8	65	......	285,000	100	60	10	10	180
48	35,000	120	9	112	......	[18] 4,000	80	60	8	9	157
49	150,000	200	12	77	......	378,000	95	70	6	8	179
50	25,000	100	7	70	......	[19] 1,000	55	60	10	7	132
51	150,000	200	17	86	5,792	600,000	215	85	....	....	300
52	100,000	150	......	......	5,280	450,000	52	60	....	....	112
53	150,000	250	13	87	......	[20] 150,000	110	70	8	10	198
54	125,000	200	12	85	......	580,000	100	70	10	14	194
Total	$6,906,000	10,371	417	3,213	91,928	17,626,388	4,761	2,507	232	238	7,738

[18] 717,500 pounds other material used.
[19] 910,000 " " " "
[20] 620,000 " " " "

WOOLEN PRODUCTION.

This table has reference to the number of yards of goods produced during the year 1897 in the fifty-four establishments represented in the tabulation as manufacturers of cloths composed wholly or in part of wool, and also exhibits the value of product per yard and in total, together with the amount paid in wages. The latter amount, for reasons which have been hereinbefore explained, appears in the aggregate only.

It will be noticed that in two instances there are no figures given stating the number of yards of goods produced. This is explained by the footnote accompanying the table. It is proper, however, to state here that the material produced by the two establishments above mentioned, while composed of wool, was not used by themselves in the manufacture of woolen goods, but entered into the finished product of other establishments. In order, then, that the average value of production per yard be accurate, the amount of the production above referred to should be deducted from the total value of manufactured product, which has been done as shown in the table.

The number of yards of goods produced by all establishments was 17,235,929. The stated value of this production was $12,176,827.67. Deducting from this amount the value of product "reported elsewhere," and the net product value of the quantity of goods reported as having been manufactured during the year 1897 was $11,887,227.67, or 69 cents per yard.

The total amount paid in wages, exclusive of salaries, during the year was $2,667,953.07. The proportion of product value paid in wages was, therefore, 22 per cent.

WOOLEN.

TABLE No. 2.— Capacity for Production.

Number of Establishment.	Yards of goods produced during 1897.	Value of product manufactured.	Value per yard.	Per cent. production of full capacity.	Value of product, full capacity.
	274,608	$68,652.00	$0.25	80	$85,815.00
2	100,000	100,000.00	1.00	100	100,000.00
3	75,000	49,920.00	.67	100	49,920.00
4	154,067	120,000.00	.78	32	375,000.00
5	115,768	175,000.00	1.51	100	175,000.00
6	150,000	162,000.00	1.08	65	249,230.77
7	321,428	450,000.09	1.40	83	542,168.92
8	80,000	140,000.00	1.75	25	560,000.00
	101,516	65,000.00	.64	100	65,000.00
10	84,836	151,766.00	1.79	60	252,943.33
11	204,853	284,264.62	1.39	83	342,487.49
12	540,000	330,000.00	.61	95	347,368.42
13	270,000	60,000.00	.22	90	66,666.66
14	120,000	240,000.00	2.00	67	358,208.96
15	221,230	339,700.00	1.54	60	566,166.67
16	360,000	664,000.00	1.84	83	800,000.00
17	520,000	200,000.00	.38	95	210,526.32
18	450,000	750,000.00	1.67	80	937,500.00
19	175,000	200,000.00	1.14	100	200,000.00
20	180,000	12,600.00	.07	50	25,200.00
21	279,122	248,637.65	.89	60	414,396.08
22	900,000	198,000.00	.22	100	198,000.0
23	160,000	200,000.00	1.25	60	333,333.33

WOOLEN — *Continued.*

TABLE No. 2.— Capacity for Production — *Continued.*

Number of Establishment.	Yards of goods produced during 1897.	Value of product manufactured.	Value per yard.	Per cent. production of full capacity.	Value of product, full capacity.
24	216,000	$125,812.00	$0.58	100	$125,812.00
25	48,707	40,000.00	.82	60	66,666.67
26	136,508	114,666.72	.84	90	127,407.47
27	450,000	250,000.00	.56	90	277,777.78
28	181,148	110,558.40	.61	66	167,512.73
29	104,000	208,000.00	2.00	95	218,947.37
30	242,396	162,106.54	.67	100	162,106.54
31	400,000	500,000.00	1.25	100	500,000.00
32	105,000	57,750.00	.55	80	72,187.50
33	90,000	65,000.00	.72	45	144,444.44
34	550,000	86,000.00	1.56	90	95,555.56
35	150,000	60,000.00	.40	83	72,289.16
36	25,000	25,000.00	1.00	33	75,757.58
37	102,500	192,187.00	1.87	100	192,187.00
38	1,296,187	1,109,306.74	.86	60	1,848,844.57
39	2,250,000	200,000.00	.09	90	222,222.22
40	240,000	140,000.00	.58	100	140,000.00
41	600,000	225,000.00	.38	100	225,000.00
42	118,300	26,400.00	.22	90	29,333.33
43	323,569	487,000.00	1.50	100	487,000.00
44	260,000	275,000.00	1.06	90	305,555.56
45	*........	25,000.00	......	100	25,000.00
46	190,169	97,500.00	.51	100	97,500.00

*Appears elsewhere.

WOOLEN—*Concluded.*

TABLE No. 2.—Capacity for Production—*Concluded.*

Number of Establishment.	Yards of goods produced during 1897.	Value of product manufactured.	Value per yard.	Per cent. production of full capacity.	Value of product, full capacity.
47	275,000	$300,000.00	$1.09	95	$315,789.47
48	799,017	218,400.00	.27	100	218,400.00
49	275,000	268,000.00	.97	85	315,294.12
50	700,000	144,000.00	.21	100	144,000.00
51	500,000	520,000.00	1.04	90	577,777.78
52	*........	264,600.00	......	100	264,600.00
53	450,000	325,000.00	.72	100	325,000.00
54	320,000	345,000.00	1.08	100	345,000.00
Total	17,235,929	†$12,176,827.67	‡$0.69	‡78	$15,439,900.80

* Appears elsewhere.
† Value of product, less goods produced, reported elsewhere, $11,887,227.07.
‡ Average.

WAGES AND RENT.

The scale of wages as shown in the tables are given by establishments only, an accurate average wage rate not being possible to obtain. As will be seen $18.20 per week was the highest wages reported as having been paid weavers, while in one instance $3.00 per week was reported as being the lowest wages paid. The highest average rate of wages reported by any establishment was $12.04 per week, the lowest average weekly wages paid weavers being $5.50.

The highest wages paid spinners was reported to have been $14.20 per week, $3.70 per week being the lowest. The highest average weekly wages paid spinners, as reported, was $12.00, and the lowest average rate $4.75 per week.

There were 1,117 tenements owned by the several manufacturers of woolen goods. The number of rooms in each ranging from three to twelve, and the rate for rent from $2.08 to $13.00 per month.

WOOLEN.

TABLE No. 3.—Wage Rates and Rates Paid for Rent.

Number of Establishment.	Weavers. Weekly wage rates.			Spinners. Weekly wage rates.			Tenements owned.	Rooms in each.	Rent per month.
	Highest.	Lowest.	Average.	Highest.	Lowest.	Average.			
1	$10.00	$6.00	$8.00	$9.00	$9.00	$9.00	9	5 to 8	$2.50 to $7.00
2	12.00	9.00	10.50	7.50	7.50	7.50	2	6 and 11	5.00 and 7.00
3	12.00	......	9.00	......	......	7.92	10	4 to 6	2.17 to 4.34
4	10.50	6.00	8.25	10.00	8.00	9.00	57	6	4.17
5	15.60	......	10.18	12.80	......	9.40	16	6 to 11	6.00 to 13.00
6	......	......	8.50	......	......	7.75	......	....	....
7	18.00	4.50	8.50	......	......	......	1	8	7.00
8	......	......	12.00	......	......	......	10	5 to 7	7.00 to 10.00
9	9.00	6.00	8.00	7.50	7.50	7.50	8	5	4.50
10	9.90	7.56	8.73	10.44	10.38	10.41	21	5	3.50
11	15.00	5.00	8.60	......	......	8.10	......	....	....
12	......	......	8.00	......	......	......	......	....	....
13	10.00	......	8.00	......	......	......	7	6	5.00
14	......	......	9.00	......	10.50	......	17	4 to 8	3.50 to 8.00
15	14.07	9.69	12.04	8.21	5.79	7.39	......	....	....
16	......	......	8.45	......	......	6.60	12	4 to 8	5.00 to 12.00
17	9.93	7.50	8.12	12.14	10.33	11.20	27	6 to 8	4.00 to 7.00
18	18.00	5.50	10.00	8.17	4.84	7.00	6	6 to 8	6.00 to 8.00
19	13.00	7.50	9.00	8.10	8.10	8.10	22	4 to 9	2.08 to 8.00
20	10.50	5.00	7.50	10.50	10.50	10.50	10	5 to 6	3.00
21	12.00	6.00	9.00	9.00	5.00	7.00	30	5	5.00
22	10.00	6.00	8.75	10.00	9.00	9.75	20	4 to 8	4.00 to 8.00
23	12.00	5.00	8.50	9.00	9.00	9.00	12	4 to 10	5.50

WOOLEN — *Continued.*

TABLE No. 3.—Wage Rates and Rates Paid for Rent — *Continued.*

Number of Establishment.	WEAVERS. Weekly wage rates.			SPINNERS. Weekly wage rates.			Tenements owned.	Rooms in each.	Rent per month.
	Highest.	Lowest.	Average.	Highest.	Lowest.	Average.			
24	$11.10	$7.65	$8.88	$11.00	$7.50	$8.46	6	4 to 5	$3.50 to $5.00
25	10.00	6.00	7.50	8.70	8.70	8.70	3	6 to 7	5.00 to 8.00
26	......	......	......	......	......	......	12	8	6.30
27	13.00	10.00	11.00	9.00	9.00	9.00	35	8	4.00
28	11.00	7.50	9.00	10.00	6.00	7.35	14	4 to 7	4.00 to 7.00
29	......	......	9.50	......	......	10.50	23	4 to 8	4.00 to 8.00
30	12.00	7.30	10.54	14.20	8.60	10.58	12	5 to 8	4.00 to 7.00
31	12.00	7.50	9.00	11.00	8.00	9.00	54	4 to 8	3.00 to 8.00
32	9.00	6.00	7.00	12.00	7.50	9.48	10	3 to 6	3.00 to 6.00
33	12.50	3.00	7.50	9.60	9.60	9.60	......	....	....
34	......	......	8.00	......	......	12.00	6	5 to 6	3.00 to 4.00
35	10.00	5.00	8.00	9.00	6.00	8.00	10	4 to 7	3.00 to 6.25
36	12.00	9.00	10.00	9.00	7.50	8.00	8	4	4.00
37	12.00	9.00	10.00	9.50	8.00	8.50	......	....	....
38	18.20	4.50	9.00	8.40	3.70	4.75	240	3 to 8	3.45 to 11.25
39	9.50	7.50	8.25	12.00	10.50	11.00	28	4 to 9	4.00 to 7.00
40	10.00	7.00	8.50	11.00	6.00	8.50	12	3 to 4	2.50 to 6.00
41	13.00	7.00	8.10	12.00	9.00	10.20	42	4 to 12	3.50 to 7.50
42	12.00	8.00	8.75	7.20	7.20	7.20	14	6	5.00
43	12.00	7.50	9.00	9.00	6.50	7.50	77	4 to 10	3.50 to 8.00
44	13.00	8.50	10.00	10.00	7.00	7.75	28	4 to 8	4.00 to 8.00
45	......	......	......	9.00	6.25	7.80	......	....	....
46	12.00	6.00	8.00	12.00	10.00	10.50	10	3 to 5	3.50 to 4.50

WOOLEN — *Concluded.*

TABLE No. 3.—Wage Rates and Rates Paid for Rent — *Concluded.*

Number of Establishment.	Weavers. Weekly wage rates.			Spinners. Weekly wage rates.			Tenements owned.	Rooms in each.	Rent per month.
	Highest.	Lowest.	Average.	Highest.	Lowest.	Average.			
47	$13.00	$9.00	$10.50	$12.00	$9.50	$11.00	......	....	....
48	13.00	5.00	6.50	13.00	9.00	10.00	9	3 to 4	$3.00 to $4.25
49	12.00	7.00	8.75	10.00	6.00	7.50	30	3 to 5	3.00 to 5.00
50	8.00	5.00	5.50	10.00	7.00	8.50	6	4 to 5	3.00 to 4.00
51	12.00	6.50	10.00	10.00	7.00	9.00	71	4 to 6	4.00 to 6.00
52	......	......	......	12.00	8.00	9.00	30	4 to 6	4.00 to 7.00
53	12.00	6.00	7.50	12.00	7.00	8.00	20	3 to 5	3.00 to 4.00
54	13.00	6.00	10.00	......	......	......	10	3 to 6	4.00 to 7.00

ASSESSMENTS AND TAXES.

The fifty-four establishments represented in the foregoing were located in twenty-eight different towns. The assessment laid against them for purposes of taxation, in 1897, was $4,549,798.00, and the amount paid by them for taxes to the several towns was $58,686.30. The average rate of taxation was 13 mills. The following table shows the amount of assessment and the amount paid in taxes, divided by towns.

WOOLEN GOODS.

Assessments and Taxes Paid, Divided by Towns.

Town.	Assessment on Grand List, 1897.	Amount paid in taxes, 1897.
Bridgeport	$110,000	$1,320.00
Coventry	12,575	188.62
East Lyme	31,450	377.40
East Windsor	205,350	3,080.25
Enfield	652,250	11,109.88
Glastonbury	81,235	1,218.52
Greenwich	69,900	908.70
Killingly	124,250	1,863.75
Ledyard	7,300	109.50
Manchester	77,799	1,166.98
Meriden	112,700	2,366.70
Middletown	15,780	157.80
Montville	20,375	326.00
Norwalk	158,500	3,170.00
Norwich	258,835	1,682.43
Plainfield	154,100	1,849.20
Preston	69,975	1,119.60
Putnam	164,151	3,118.87
Seymour	74,000	1,480.00
Somers	113,205	1,358.46
Sprague	6,300	94.50
Stafford	275,559	5,511.18
Stonington	14,000	175.00

WOOLEN GOODS — *Concluded.*

Assessments and Taxes Paid, Divided by Towns — *Concluded.*

Town.	Assessment on Grand List, 1897.	Amount paid in taxes, 1897.
Thompson	$37,075	$444.90
Torrington	98,000	1,372.00
Winchester	5,000	65.00
Woodbury	35,712	535.68
Vernon	1,564,422	12,515.38
Total	$4,549,798	$58,686.30

CLOSED MILLS.

There were found to be in the State fifteen establishments which had been engaged in the manufacture of woolen goods previous to the period covered by this investigation. These establishments, when in operation, had 79 sets of cards in use and 543 looms in operation, and were assessed in the grand list of 1897 at $183,826.00, and paid $3,113.25 in taxes to the different towns in which they were located. Three of the establishments reported as being "closed mills" were not assessed for purposes of taxation, and although they appear in the tabulation referring to sets of cards and number of looms, no reference is made to the locality of the mills in the exhibit of assessment and taxes paid to towns.

WOOLENS — Closed Mills.

Table No. 3. — Capacity for Production.

Number of Establishment.	Sets of cards.	Number of looms.
55	8	54
56	17	101
57	4	20
58	1	4
59	1	8
60	5	37
61	2	16
62	5	38
63	......	2
64	4	56
65	5	28
66	11	56
67	8	40
68	1	3
69	7	80
Total	79	543

WOOLEN GOODS — Closed Mills.

Assessments and Taxes Paid, Divided by Towns.

Town.	Assessment on Grand List, 1897.	Amount paid in taxes, 1897.
Bethlehem	$6,111	$48.89
Coventry	23,800	357.00
Eastford	1,000	16.00
Montville	2,900	46.40
New London	20,000	640.00
Newtown	15,180	166.98
Norwalk	38,000	760.00
Norwich	32,800	328.00
Southbury	500	7.50
Sprague	25,643	384.64
Stafford	10,000	200.00
Willington	7,892	157.84
Total	$183,826	$3,113.25

ILLUSTRATIONS.

The following exhibits are made up from the returns made by ten manufacturing establishments, the product of which consisted of broadcloths, cassimeres, cloakings, woolens and worsteds, and have been prepared for the purpose of showing the proportion of product value which was paid for wages, and also to show the average number of yards produced per loom and per employe, by establishments.

The same explanation should apply to these illustrations as has been made in the preceding chapter concerning the cotton industry.

A most interesting comparison can here be made with the figures contained in the report of the Commissioner of Industrial and Labor Statistics for the State of Maine which has just been issued, and covers the same period as does this report. The publication referred to gives the statistics from twenty-five establishments engaged in the manufacture of woolen goods. The total value of product of these establishments in 1897 was $3,630,312, and the total amount paid in wages $911,037. The proportion of product value paid in wages was 25 per cent.

Making comparisons with the ten establishments in Connecticut shown in the following exhibits, it is found that the total value of product of these was $2,406,616.62, and the amount paid by them in wages $571,962.73, this being 24 per cent. of product value.

It must be remembered, however, in making comparisons that the proportion of product value paid in wages by the fifty-four establishments covered by this investigation was 22 per cent.

EXHIBIT 1.

Year 1897.
36 looms, 2 sets of cards,
Produced 274,608 yards cassimeres.
Average number employed, 58.
Average yards produced per loom, 7,628.
Average yards produced per employe, 4,735.
Value of product, $68,652.00.
Amount paid in wages, $18,792.09.
Per cent. of product value paid in wages, 27.4.

EXHIBIT 2.

Year 1897.
21 looms, 2 sets of cards,
Produced 100,000 yards fancy worsteds.
Average number employed, 52.
Average yards produced per loom, 4,762.
Average yards produced per employe, 1,923.
Value of product, $100,000.
Amount paid in wages, $18,000.00.
Per cent. of product value paid in wages, 18.

EXHIBIT 3.

Year 1897.
22 looms, 5 sets of cards,
Produced 115,768 yards wool uniform cloths.
Average number employed, 79.
Average yards produced per loom, 5,262.
Average yards produced per employe, 1,465.
Value of product, $175,000.00.
Amount paid in wages, $32,525.90.
Per cent. of product value paid in wages, 18.6.

EXHIBIT 4.

Year 1897.
109 looms, 9 sets of cards,
Produced 321,428 yards cassimeres and worsteds
Average number employed, 311.
Average yards produced per loom, 2,949.
Average yards produced per employe, 1,034.
Value of product, $450,000.00.
Amount paid in wages, $122,142.83.
Per cent. of product value paid in wages, 27.1.

EXHIBIT 5.

Year 1897.
20 looms, 4 sets of cards,
Produced 101,516 yards cassimeres and cloakings.
Average number employed, 44.
Average yards produced per loom, 5,076.
Average yards produced per employe, 2,307.
Value of product, $65,000.00.
Amount paid in wages, $15,525.00.
Per cent. of product value paid in wages, 23.9.

EXHIBIT 6.

Year 1897.
76 looms, 15 sets of cards,
Produced 204,853 yards woolens, worsteds and cassimeres.
Average number employed, 252.
Average yards produced per loom, 2,695.
Average yards produced per employe, 813.
Value of product, $284,264.62.
Amount paid in wages, $71,935.12.
Per cent. of product value paid in wages, 25.3.

EXHIBIT 7.

Year 1897.
28 looms, 3 sets of cards,
Produced 270,000 yards union cassimeres.
Average number employed, 48.
Average yards produced per loom, 9,643.
Average yards produced per employe, 5,625.
Value of product, $60,000.00.
Amount paid in wages, $17,000.00.
Per cent. of product value paid in wages, 28.3.

EXHIBIT 8.

Year 1897.
125 looms, 20 sets of cards,
Produced 221,230 yards fine worsteds and woolens.
Average number employed, 299.
Average yards produced per loom, 1,770,
Average yards produced per employe, 740.
Value of product, $339,700.00.
Amount paid in wages, $96,489.79.
Per cent. of product value paid in wages, 28.4.

EXHIBIT 9.

Year 1897.
160 looms, 9 sets of cards,
Produced 360,000 yards woolens and worsteds.
Average number employed, 375.
Average yards produced per loom, 2,250.
Average yards produced per employe, 960.
Value of product, $664,000.00.
Amount paid in wages, $136,500.00.
Per cent. of product value paid in wages, 20.6.

EXHIBIT 10.

Year 1897.

54 looms, 10 sets of cards,

Produced 520,000 yards carriage and broad cloth.

Average number employed, 114.

Average yards produced per loom, 9,630.

Average yards produced per employe, 4,561.

Value of product, $200,000.00.

Amount paid in wages, $43,052.00.

Per cent. of product value paid in wages, 21.5.

KNIT GOODS.

Classified as manufacturers of knit goods are those establishments the product of which consists of hosiery, men's, women's and infants' underwear, the material used being made up of both cotton and wool. Accurate division of this material being impossible, the quantity used is given in the aggregate and includes all material used in the process of manufacture except the amount of cotton yarn purchased of other manufacturers, the amount of the material for the manufacture of which appears in the table referring to cotton warps, webs, threads and yarns.

There were twenty-three establishments in operation in the State during the year 1897. The amount of capital invested (exclusive of surplus) being $1,863,000.00. The number of cards reported as being in use was 126 sets. There was also in operation in all the establishments shown in the tabulation 38 looms, 53,514 spindles and 1,204 knitting and other machines. It should be stated that one establishment was reported as being closed, the capacity of which was 11 sets of cards and 45 machines, thus making the total number of cards 137, and 1,249 machines, total capacity for production being considered.

The total amount of material used (exclusive of cotton yarns purchased) was 5,451,392 pounds. The average number of persons employed during the year was 3,006, of which 913 were men, 1,921 women, 68 boys and 104 girls, the two last named classes being under 16 years of age. The proportion of children of total number employed, therefore, was 5.7 per cent.

The production of all the establishments for the year covered by the investigation amounted to 706,964 dozen of the various kinds of hosiery and knit goods, in addition to which there was manufactured 100,000 square yards and 348,000 pounds of other goods, the nature of which was such as to render it impossible to classify as to number of pieces.

The total value of product manufactured by these establishments during the year 1897 was $3,630,550.52, and the amount paid in wages (exclusive of salaries) for the same period $967,752.47, this being 26.7 per cent. of product value.

WAGES AND RENT.

As previously stated, the actual average wage rate was not obtainable, the highest and lowest average only can be given, which were, for knitters $11.00 and $4.50 per week, respectively, and to spinners the highest average rate paid was $14.40 and the lowest $7.15 per week.

There were 137 tenements reported as being owned by the several establishments, the number of rooms in each ranging from 4 to 10, and the rate paid for rent from $3.00 to $12.00 per month.

ASSESSMENTS AND TAXES.

The total assessment laid against all establishments for purposes of taxation, by the towns in which these industries were located, was $1,505,528; and the amount paid in taxes $21,134.47, the average rate of tax being 14 mills.

KNIT GOODS.

TABLE NO. 1. — Capacity for Production.

Number of Establishment.	Capital invested.	Horse power.	Sets of cards.	Number of looms.	Number of machines.	Number of spindles.	Pounds of material used.	Average number employed during 1897.				
								Men.	Women.	Boys.	Girls.	Total.
1	$30,000	280	......	......	80	6,000	55,000	25	60	3	......	88
2	13,000	6	......	......	40	....	*.........	2	34	......	......	36
3	40,000	20	......	......	18	....	*13,000	10	26	......	......	36
4	15,000	3	......	....	24	....	*........	2	20	......	......	22
5	2,000	6	......	......	12	....	*........	5	......	......	......	5
6	150,000	120	11	......	50	2,640	212,000	50	100	......	5	155
7	50,000	70	3	.....	25	768	32,000	17	33	......	......	50
8	300,000	300	20	.....	....	9,500	261,572	124	328	6	17	475
9	150,000	150	13	.....	72	2,600	150,000	40	100	25	30	195
10	125,000	150	9	......	60	3,264	287,500	50	125	3	3	181
11	100,000	125	5	......	125	566	360,000	40	120	5	10	175
12	75,000	125	8	......	32	2,040	240,000	40	100	1	6	147
13	40,000	125	10	10	37	2,736	475,127	93	71	2	2	168
14	60,000	300	6	12	68	2,496	176,000	30	40	6	6	82
15	50,000	150	8	16	....	2,100	300,000	40	70	......	......	110
16	350,000	200	13	......	185	4,500	1,500,000	150	250	......	......	400
17	8,000	25	1	......	6	....	53,000	2	5	......	......	7
18	60,000	100	7	......	67	2,304	123,300	50	116	6	10	182
19	50,000	75	7	......	60	1,800	189,893	45	75	......	......	120
20	80,000	200	......	......	115	3,000	360,000	35	120	5	7	167
21	60,000	150	5	. ....	24	2,200	278,000	28	80	3	5	116
22	5,000	3	......	......	18	....	*........	1	10	......	......	11
23	50,000	150	......	......	86	5,000	385,000	34	38	3	3	78
Total	$1,863,000	2,833	126	38	1,204	53,514	5,451,392	913	1,921	68	104	3,006

Closed Establishments.

1	....	....	11	......	45	....	....	......	......	......	......	......

* Yarns purchased.

KNIT GOODS.

Table No. 2.—Capacity for Production.

Number of Establishment.	Dozens of goods produced during 1897.	Value of product manufactured.	Per cent. production of full capacity.	Value of product, full capacity.
1	5,000	$66,000.00	25	$264,000.00
2	15,000	30,000.00	75	40,000.00
3	20,000	64,000.00	75	85,333.33
4	25,000	24,000.00	100	24,000.00
5	12,000	4,750.00	75	6,333.33
6	34,254	70,000.00	60	116,666.67
7	25,000	26,000.00	60	43,333.33
8	47,000	460,000.00	50	920,000.00
9	67,000	100,000.00	60	166,666.67
10	14,000	250,000.00	85	294,117.65
11	65,000	275,000.00	96	286,458.33
12	28,000	140,000.00	80	175,000.00
13	36,857	300,642.56	95	316,465.95
14	8,500	63,000.00	68	92,647.06
15	40,000	280,000.00	100	280,000.00
16	75,000	425,000.00	100	425,000.00
17	*.......	10,000.00	60	16,666.67
18	56,000	220,000.00	100	220,000.00
19	13,753	286,657.96	61	469,931.08
20	60,000	240,000.00	95	252,631.58
21	58,000	135,000.00	100	135,000.00
22	1,600	6,500.00	33	19,696.97
23	†.......	154,000.00	60	256,666.67
Total	706,964	$3,630,550.52	74	$4,906,615.29

* 100,000 square yards.
† 348,000 pounds

KNIT GOODS.

TABLE NO. 3. — Wage Rates and Rates Paid for Rent.

Number of Establishment.	Knitters. Weekly wage rates.			Spinners. Weekly wage rates.			Tenements owned.	Rooms in each.	Rent per month.
	Highest.	Lowest.	Average.	Highest.	Lowest.	Average.			
1	$12.00	$4.20	$7.20	$12.00	$6.60	$7.40	13	5	$5.00
2	10.00	6.00	7.00	......	......	......	......	....	....
3	10.50	10.50	10.50	......	......	......	......	....	....
4	10.00	6.00	7.50	......	......	......	......	....	....
5	8.00	5.00	6.00	......	......	......	......	....	....
6	12.00	5.40	7.50	12.00	9.00	10.00	......	....	....
7	8.10	6.90	7.50	12.00	9.00	10.50	6	7	3.00 to 6.00
8	......	......	......	12.00	7.00	10.00	......	....	....
9	......	......	......	10.00	6.60	8.10	2	....	8.00
10	10.00	5.00	8.00	8.00	6.00	7.50	25	5 to 10	5.00 to 12.00
11	9.00	6.90	8.10	10.80	6.60	8.70	1	7	6.00
12	12.00	9.00	9.50	12.00	10.00	10.50	7	7	9.00
13	11.00	9.00	10.00	11.00	9.00	10.00	37	4 to 8	4.00 to 9.00
14	8.00	7.00	7.50	7.50	6.75	7.15	12	6	4.50
15	10.50	6.00	8.00	12.00	6.00	7.50	......	....	....
16	12.00	7.50	11.00	12.00	7.50	11.00	34	4 to 5	Average 10.00
17	6.00	6.00	6.00	......	......	......	......	....	....
18	12.00	9.00	10.50	16.50	12.00	14.40	......	....	....
19	12.00	9.00	9.50	12.00	9.00	9.50	......	....	....
20	12.00	7.00	10.50	12.00	7.00	10.50	......	....	....
21	12.00	8.10	11.00	12.00	8.10	11.00	......	....	....
22	6.00	3.00	4.50	......	......	......	......	....	....
23	......	......	......	12.00	8.50	11.25	......	....	....

KNIT GOODS.

Assessments and Taxes Paid, Divided by Towns.

Town.	Assessment on Grand List, 1897.	Amount paid in taxes, 1897.
Bridgeport	$11,000	$132.00
Bristol	100,610	1,226.61
Derby	296,533	2,668.79
Glastonbury	50,125	721.87
Hartford	6,500	130.00
Huntington	60,000	660.00
Madison	400	4.00
Manchester	34,400	516.00
Naugatuck	8,225	119.26
New Britain	417,000	8,340.00
New Haven	10,000	240.00
Norfolk	22,000	264.00
Plainville	80,476	724.28
Stamford	4,125	86.62
Sterling	39,900	518.70
Trumbull	1,900	22.80
Vernon	60,000	480.00
Waterbury	50,000	1,400.00
Windsor	14,000	182.00
Windsor Locks	133,600	1,336.00
Winchester	104,734	1,361.54
Total	$1,505,528	$21,134.47

SILK GOODS.

The silk manufacturing industry in Connecticut is a very important one, and the nature of the product is such that to undertake to describe in detail the different kinds or varieties of goods produced, or to endeavor to show the number of yards, pieces or pounds manufactured would, in a greater or less degree, violate the agreements made with the establishments that have furnished the Bureau with detailed information, and for this reason the table referring to silk goods contains only the data secured which shows the capital invested (not including accumulation or surplus) by firm, individual or corporation engaged in the business in 1897. The table also shows the number of horse power used by the several establishments, the number of pounds of silk consumed in the process of manufacture, the value of manufactured product, the amount paid in wages (aggregate only), and the average number employed by all establishments, together with the average weekly wage rate paid weavers and spinners.

Information was secured from twenty-five establishments engaged in the silk industry, which were in operation in 1897. The aggregate amount of capital invested in these (exclusive of surplus) was $4,008,000.00. 1,607,150 pounds of silk were consumed in the process of manufacture, the value of manufactured product being $7,488,485.05, and the amount paid in wages (exclusive of salaries) $1,734,739, this amount being 23 per cent. of product value. The total average number employed in all establishments was 5,154, of which 2,093 were men, 2,590 women and 471 boys and girls under 16 years of age. 9.1 per cent. of the total number employed, therefore, being children.

The highest average wages paid weavers was found to be $15.00 per week; the lowest average being $7.50 per week. $10.00 per week was the highest average wage rate paid spinners, and the lowest $4.50 per week.

SILK.

TABLE NO. 1.— Capacity for Production.

Number of Establishment.	Capital invested.	Horse power.	Pounds of silk used in 1897.	Value of product manufactured.	Average number employed during 1897.					Average weekly wage rate.	
					Men.	Women.	Boys.	Girls.	Total.	Weavers.	Spinners.
1	$12,000	30	10,000	$24,000.00	3	16	1	......	20	......	$6.75
2	50,000	70	3,000	40,000.00	......	50	2	3	55	$7.50	......
3	100,000	80	41,523	91,496.25	23	72	......	......	95	......	7.50
4	1,000,000	140	88,650	926,000.00	35	200	30	20	285	......	7.75
5	20,000	40	15,000	100,000.00	15	30	10	10	65	......	7.00
6	145,000	100	25,000	150,000.00	25	100	......	......	125	7.50	7.00
7	6,000	15	6,533	21,492.00	3	7	......	2	12	......	9.25
8	150,000	30	28,000	250,000.00	50	52	7	......	109	......	10.00
9	25,000	40	13,553	106,000.00	18	42	......	......	60	......	8.75
10	15,000	20	7,500	30,000.00	5	15	......	......	20	......	7.25
11	60,000	150	60,892	200,000.00	12	90	......	......	102	......	7.50
12	640,000	150	22,948	231,226.48	80	125	7	......	212	15.00	......
13	15,000	15	17,539	70,156.00	10	43	5	4	62	......	7.50
14	60,000	25	*150	65,000.00	10	20	......	......	30	13.00	......
15	25,000	25	12,000	50,000.00	48	13	2	2	65	13.25	......
16	75,000	150	65,000	200,000.00	100	50	......	......	150	11.50	......
17	100,000	250	100,000	600,000.00	240	160	30	40	470	11.00	......
18	50,000	30	30,000	150,000.00	5	50	......	......	55	......	6.25
19	1,000,000	1,850	*750,362	3,139,211.32	1,096	855	75	139	2,165	8.70	7.50
20	60,000	75	11,500	150,000.00	27	130	4	8	169	9.00	4.50
21	60,000	100	3,000	33,903.00	35	35	......	......	70	10.00	4.60
22	100,000	125	95,000	375,000.00	150	150	10	10	320	11.50	......
23	100,000	100	65,000	170,000.00	50	120	4	4	178	......	7.00
24	15,000	50	35,000	65,000.00	8	40	6	6	60	......	7.25
25	125,000	200	100,000	250,000.00	45	125	15	15	200	......	8.50
Total	$4,008,000	3,860	1,607,150	$7,488,485.05	2,093	2,590	208	263	5,154	......	......

* Other material purchased.

Total amount paid in wages, all establishments, $1,734,739.
Proportion wages paid of product value, 23 per cent.

	Value of product manufactured.	Per cent. production of full capacity.	Value of product, full capacity.
All establishments..............	$7,488,485.05	†77	$9,725,777.28

† Average.

ASSESSMENTS AND TAXES.

As will be seen by referring to the preceding table, there were twenty-five establishments in the State actively engaged in the manufacture of silk goods in 1897. It should be noted, however, that there were two establishments reported as being closed during that period.

The total number of establishments against which assessments for purposes of taxation were laid was, therefore, twenty-seven. These were located in twenty-two different towns, as will be seen by the following table. The total amount of assessment laid (including assessments against closed mills), was $2,292,381, and the amount paid in taxes to the several towns by all establishments was $35,166.36. The average rate of taxation was 15 mills.

SILK GOODS.

Assessments and Taxes Paid, Divided by Towns.

Town.	Assessment on Grand List, 1897.	Amount paid in taxes, 1897.
Bridgeport	$150,100	$1,801.20
Coventry	4,025	60.37
Danbury	15,550	311.00
Hamden	3,050	45.75
Hartford	70,000	1,400.00
Hebron	31,900	446.60
Manchester	1,421,561	21,323.41
Mansfield	3,252	48.78
New Haven	6,500	156.00
New London	110,400	3,532.80
Norfolk	15,000	180.00
Norwalk	2,500	50.00
Norwich	28,500	470.20
Preston	13,000	208.00
Putnam	31,000	589.00
Stonington	14,720	331.20
Vernon	151,000	1,208.00
Watertown	119,823	1,318.05
Winchester	45,000	585.00
Windham	37,000	851.00
Windsor Locks	5,500	55.00
Total	$2,279,381	$34,971.36

Closed Mills.

Mansfield	$1,000	$15.00
Marlborough	12,000	180.00
Total	$13,000	$195.00

SUMMARY.

A summary of the foregoing is presented herewith and shows, in a condensed form, the results of the work of the Bureau in the investigation of the subject of the condition of the textile industries in the State.

It will be noted that in the case of the silk industry the mechanical appliances used in manufacture and the quantity of goods produced, has been omitted from the tabulation. The reason for this omission has been explained elsewhere. The value of product and the total amount paid in wages is given, however, thus indicating the per cent. of product value paid in wages.

RECAPITULATION.

Goods Manufactured.	Number of establishments considered.	Number of horse power.	Capital invested, 1897.	Value of product manufactured, 1897.	Amount paid in wages, 1897.	Per cent. wages paid of product value.	Average per cent. production of full capacity.	Value of product, full capacity.	Average number employed. Males.	Females.
Cotton	60	30,499	$15,671,700	$15,540,534.42	$4,830,023.37	31.1	80	$17,426,869.45	7,767	7,870
Woolen	54	10,871	6,906,000	11,887,227.67	2,067,958.07	22.	78	15,439,900.80	4,993	2,745
Knit	24	2,833	1,863,000	8,630,550.52	967,752.47	26.7	74	4,906,615.29	981	2,025
Silk	25	3,360	4,008,000	7,488,485.05	1,784,739.00	23.	77	9,725,777.28	2,301	2,853
Total	163	47,563	$28,448,700	$38,546,797.66	$10,200,467.91	26.5	81	$47,499,162.82	16,042	15,493

Goods Manufactured.	Sets of cards in use, 1897.	Looms in operation, 1897.	Machines in use, 1897.	Spindles in operation, 1897.	Cards idle, 1897.	Looms idle, 1897.	Machines idle, 1897.	Spindles idle, 1897.	Total number. Cards.	Looms.	Machines.	Spindles.
Cotton	.....	21,080	.....	1,038,020	.....	794	.....	56,048	.....	21,874	.....	1,094,068
Woolen	417	3,213	.....	91,928	79	543	.....	.....	496	3,756	.....	91,928
Knit	126	38	1,204	53,514	11	....	45	.....	137	38	1,249	53,514
Total	543	24,331	1,204	1,183,462	90	1,337	45	56,048	633	25,668	1,249	1,239,510

RECAPITULATION—*Concluded.*

Goods Manufactured.	Pounds of cotton used in 1897.	Pounds of wool used in 1897.	Pounds of silk used in 1897.	Pounds of other material used in 1897.	Yards of goods produced in 1897.	Dozens of goods produced in 1897.	Pounds of goods produced in 1897.
Cotton	53,104,000	....	....	5,000	204,214,178	2,286,532	7,486,951
Woolen	....	17,626,388	....	4,041,171	17,235,929	....	....
Knit	....	....	....	*5,451,392	100,000	706,964	348,000
Silk	....	....	1,607,150	....	....	....	....
Total	53,104,000	17,626,388	1,607,150	9,497,563	221,550,107	2,993,496	7,834,951

* Exclusive of yarns purchased.

Goods Manufactured.	Total assessment on Grand List, 1897.	Total amount paid in taxes, 1897.	Number of tenements owned.	Rooms in each.	Rate of rent per month.	Average weekly wages.					
						Weavers.		Spinners.		Knitters.	
						Highest.	Lowest.	Highest.	Lowest.	Highest.	Lowest.
Cotton	$10,870,519	$147,209.75	3,084	2 to 10	$ .90 to $11.00	$18.00	$5.00	$12.00	$4.00	......	......
Woolen	4,733,624	61,799.55	1,117	3 to 12	2.08 to 13.00	12.04	5.50	12.00	4.75	......	......
Knit	1,505,528	21,134.47	187	4 to 10	3.00 to 12.00	......	......	14.40	7.15	$11.00	$4.50
Silk	2,292,381	35,166.36	......	......	....	15.00	7.50	10.00	4.50	......	......
Total	$18,902,052	$265,310.13	4,388	......	....	......	......	......	......	......	......

In closing the portion of this report devoted to the subject of the manufactures of textiles in Connecticut, an interesting comparison can be made with existing conditions in North Carolina, the material for which is taken from the report of the Bureau of Labor Statistics of that State for the year 1897.

It appears in the publication referred to that in the year named there were 208 establishments in the State engaged in the manufacture of cotton and hosiery goods, with 24,517 looms, 1,044,385 spindles and 1,410 machines in operation, requiring the use of 43,000 horse power in running the plants.

The largest number of looms in operation in any one establishment was 1,366, and of spindles 28,350. The largest amount of capital invested in any one establishment is reported as being $500,000.

The total number employed in these mills was 25,887, of which 5,363 or 20.7 per cent. were children.

Comparisons made with the conditions which obtain in the establishments manufacturing similar goods in Connecticut make it apparent that conditions are more favorable in this State than in the South, for the investigation made by this Bureau into the prevailing conditions here develops the information that in the same year as was covered by the report of the Bureau of Labor Statistics of North Carolina there was found to be 84 establishments actively engaged in the manufacture of cotton and hosiery goods in this State, having 21,118 looms, 1,091,534 spindles and 1,204 machines in operation during the year. The horse power required for the running of these establishments was 33,332. The largest number of looms in use in any one establishment was 2,947 and of spindles 118,938. In amount of capital $2,000,000 was the largest invested in any establishment.

In the matter of employes there was a total number of 18,643 engaged in all the establishments which were in operation, 1,724 or 9.2 per cent. being children. Obviously, the laws governing the employment of children in the factories of Connecticut are beneficent ones, and in comparison to the conditions as they exist in North Carolina (where there is no age limit for the employment of children) are operating in the interests of the working classes, and in no way detrimental to the interests of manufacturers.

In this connection it is interesting and appropriate to make the following extract from the report of the North Carolina Bureau of Labor Statistics, comment being unnecessary and superfluous:

"The wages of our cotton operatives are much lower than the wages paid in the mills of the North, and while the Northern States have passed laws regulating the hours of labor in the factory, our State has let the matter rest on the same basis as on the farm, in the mine and in the forest."

Further information gleaned from the same report develops the rather interesting fact that the average hours of labor in the mills of this one of the Southern group of textile manufacturing States are 69 per week, while in Connecticut the average is but 60 hours per week, and as affecting the employment of women and children it is unlawful in this State "that the hours of labor exceed sixty in a week."

Another most interesting comparison can be made as to the number of spindles operated by the employes in the two States considered, for it appears that in North Carolina there were employed 25,887 persons for the operation of 1,044,385 spindles, this being 40.34 spindles per person employed, while in Connecticut, where the hours of labor are nine hours per week less than in North Carolina, the average number of spindles operated per employe was 58.55. It should be borne in mind that this comparison has been made with establishments in both States which were engaged in the manufacture of cotton goods and hosiery. It must also be borne in mind that the percentage of children of total number employed is much less in Connecticut than in North Carolina, which may account in a measure for this wide discrepancy in number of spindles operated per employe.

The hours of labor which prevail in the States in which the manufacturing industries consist largely of textiles is an important factor, and the following synopsis of the laws which have been enacted is herewith presented.

SYNOPSIS OF THE LAWS RELATING TO THE HOURS OF LABOR AND THE EMPLOYMENT OF WOMEN AND CHILDREN.

NEW ENGLAND STATES—SOUTHERN STATES.

EMPLOYMENT OF CHILDREN.

NEW ENGLAND STATES.

CONNECTICUT.—

No child under fourteen years of age shall be employed in any mechanical, mercantile or manufacturing establishment. None shall be employed between fourteen and sixteen years of age who cannot read and write unless they produce a certificate from a teacher of an evening school that they have attended eighteen consecutive sessions of the current month. Inspection of establishments is made by agents of the State Board of Education. Penalty for violation not more than sixty dollars. Each week of employment to be considered a separate offence.*

MAINE.—

If under twelve years of age children may be employed if at school taught by a qualified teacher for four months of each year preceding time of employment. Under fifteen years of age, three months under same conditions. Penalty for violation is $100. School committee investigates and reports to County attorney who shall prosecute.

NEW HAMPSHIRE.—

None to be employed under ten years of age. None under sixteen years of age to be employed that cannot read and

*Eleven prosecutions for violations were brought during the current year, nine of which were for illegal employment in Textile manufactories.

write, during the time the public schools are in session in the district in which they reside. If under sixteen years of age and over fourteen years, they must furnish certificate of twelve weeks' attendance at school. If under fourteen and over twelve years of age, six months or such portion of time as schools may be open. If under twelve and over ten years of age they must attend all the time the schools are open.

Penalty not to exceed $50 for each offence. Duty of school board to prosecute. Failure on their part to do so subjects them to penalty of $20 for each neglect.

VERMONT.—

None under ten years of age. Over ten and under fourteen years of age may be employed when in possession of certificate showing attendance at public school of twenty weeks during year preceding employment. Penalty not less than $5 and not more than $25. Inspection and prosecution by truant officer.

MASSACHUSETTS.—

None to be employed under thirteen years of age. Between thirteen and fourteen years of age may be employed during vacation of public schools, if in possession of certificate showing thirty weeks' attendance at school during year preceding employment. Penalty not less than $20 and not more than $50. None can be employed under fourteen years of age who cannot read and write the English language. Inspection by truant officer, who may prosecute.

RHODE ISLAND.—

None to be employed under twelve years of age. None over twelve and under fifteen while the public schools are in session who cannot write his or her name, age and place of residence legibly. Between twelve and fifteen years of age children may be employed if in possession of certificate showing eighty days' attendance at school or certificate showing that they have acquired the elementary branches taught in the public schools. May also be excused by school committee.

SOUTHERN STATES.

ALABAMA.—

No limit in manufacturing. In mines none allowed under ten years of age.

GEORGIA.—

No limit.

NORTH CAROLINA.—

No limit.

SOUTH CAROLINA.—

No limit.

TENNESSEE.—

In factories and mines none under twelve years of age. Penalty not less than $50 and not more than $500.

VIRGINIA.—

No limit.

KENTUCKY.—

No limit.

MISSISSIPPI.—

No limit.

HOURS OF LABOR.

NEW ENGLAND STATES.

CONNECTICUT.—

No minor under sixteen years of age, and no woman shall be employed more than sixty hours per week.

NEW HAMPSHIRE.—

No minor under eighteen years of age, and no woman shall be employed more than sixty hours per week.

VERMONT.—

No one under fifteen years of age shall be employed more than sixty hours per week.

MASSACHUSETTS.—

No woman or minor under eighteen years of age shall be employed between hours of 10 P. M. and 6 A. M., nor more than fifty-eight hours per week.

MAINE.—

No woman or minor under sixteen years of age shall be employed more than sixty hours per week.

RHODE ISLAND.—

No woman or minor under eighteen years of age shall be employed more than sixty hours per week. Penalty not exceeding $20 for each offence.

SOUTHERN STATES.

ALABAMA.—

No limit.

GEORGIA.—

Minors (under twenty-one years of age), sunrise to sunset. In cotton or woolen mills sixty-six hours per week. Penalty not less than $20 and not more than $500 for each offence.

NORTH CAROLINA.—

No limit.

SOUTH CAROLINA.—

Sixty-six hours per week; may be seventy hours to make up for lost time. Penalty not less than $50 and not more than $100 for each offence.

TENNESSEE.—

No limit.

VIRGINIA.—

No minor under fourteen years of age, and no woman shall be employed more than sixty hours per week. Penalty not less than $5 and not more than $20.

KENTUCKY.—

No limit.

MISSISSIPPI.—

No limit.

PART II.

ORGANIZED LABOR IN CONNECTICUT.

1. Wages.
2. Hours of Labor.
3. Benefits.

ORGANIZED LABOR IN CONNECTICUT.

No question of social economy occupies a more deservedly prominent place in the thoughts of the people than does the labor movement of the day. In all the cities of the State there are found, bonded together, fellow craftsmen in many of the various trades. In order that the purposes of these associations may be known and understood, a careful investigation of their condition and needs has been undertaken, and its results are set forth in the following pages. The "workingmen" of Connecticut appear at every session of our General Assembly, advocating the passage of laws which they assert are for the betterment of their condition. The laws which have already been passed, such as those providing for factory inspection, clean bake-shops, limitation of the hours of labor, and weekly payment of wages, are the result of concerted movement by the organized labor of the State. Concerning the labor movement as it now exists, Hon. Carroll D. Wright, United States Commissioner of Labor, in an address before the National Association of Labor Commissioners, said:

"The labor question occupies a different position each succeeding decade or generation. What it may have been once does not indicate what it is now. Formerly the labor question was a very narrow one, and consisted simply in the proposition, How can wages be raised or the working hours per day reduced? And the demand of the wage-worker in former times was for an increase of wages, or a decrease in the hours of labor, or both, with a view to elevating his standard of life. You should remember that when this demand was first made wages were paid in accordance with David Ricardo's old and well known 'iron law of wages,' under which the rate of wages was fixed at a point which simply covered the absolute physical necessities of a man, his clothing, his food and his shelter. This much was to be granted for day labor, simply that the physical machine, the working anatomy, should not depreciate in value;

but in the last generation or two there has come something beyond this which means more than the mere physical wants of man, and this something else relates to the workingman's interest in society, how he can receive wages enough to enable him to become what he has been made everywhere, a political, a social, and a moral factor in the community. He now receives in wages from 10 to 15 per cent. margin above the rate which the 'iron law of wages' would fix as his compensation for so much labor rendered. This extra demand for some of the elevating and spiritualizing influences of life lies at the bottom of the labor question to-day; and so it means sociology as a whole, the science of society—how can society grow, and grow in the very best way, so that all men shall receive something of the things in this life which mean culture, education—art, even.

"This demand wherever you meet it is evidenced by what we call 'social unrest,' and it is the function of these offices which we represent to contribute facts, and facts only, which shall help us to understand the meaning of this social unrest and enable us to determine, if possible, whether there shall be any danger in it, or whether the social unrest means something that shall carry civilization still farther up in the advance of the times. Then what is the labor question concretely stated? The underlying factors of the labor question had their origin so long ago, that history gives no account of them, as far back as when a certain tribe lived on the table lands of Central Asia, away back of the historic period, and so far back that all we know of it comes from the Sanscrit. This tribe grew refined; it became intelligent; it built boats, and steered them in the streams with a rudder, and propelled them with oars as we do to-day; it wove cloth; it did many things that indicate a higher sense of true civilization; and then, gentlemen, commenced that great fever of unrest, which has followed the Aryan race to this moment, and will follow it until the end, whenever that may be, thousands or millions of years hence, and it is to this unrest that our Western Hemisphere owes its existence as a populated land. As soon as this tribe, that grew somewhat refined, found itself in that position, the ambition seized its members and a portion of the old tribe came down from the table lands of Central Asia and found itself wandering westward. Other sections came down behind them and pushed on those that were in advance, and they crossed the eastern waters and settled the Hellenic States. They made Central Europe what it is, and finally, crossed the English Channel and settled Great Britain, and soon they found themselves fretting on the outmost western rock of the Irish coast, with just as much unrest in their souls as they ever had during the centuries back of them, and they peered into the western ocean and finally one of their number, one day in October, in 1492, found himself still peering from the deck of his battered little caravel into the west, and this great continent was discovered. More of his tribe kept sweeping on and sweeping on, settling a fringe all along the Atlantic coast, crossing the rivers, and finding themselves at last beyond the Mississippi, until now the sons of this old, ambitious Aryan race are fretting on the outmost western coast of this country. Whether or not they will in time sweep over the Pacific and reach again the table lands of Central Asia, is a great question in sociology, but my reason for referring to this fact is to show you that the unrest which made this country what it is, is of the remotest origin, and we Americans find in our veins to-day the very life blood which made those characters thousands of years ago distinctive, and this unrest has followed us, and is following us, and we are feeling it in accessions as the generations pile up in the passage of time.

"This, gentlemen, concretely, is the labor question of to-day. What shall be done with this unrest; how shall it be shaped; not whether it can be killed, but whether the struggle under it can be softened, can be guided, can be moulded into some force which shall mean the very best for human conditions. * * * * * There is a great deal of pathetic talk about unrest, about discontent, and there are several kinds of discontent which prevail; but the discontent that is legitimate is that which impels men, always and ever, to seek better conditions. That is what has brought millions across the stormy western ocean to settle in this land; that is what has made the United States what it is; that is what is building the South into a great industrial empire. Now as facts are collected, classified, and systemized, we find that out of them all, which means the knowledge of conditions as they are, there is growing a new political economy. * * * * * Dr. William T. Harris, the Commissioner of Education, has defined a crank. He says a crank is a man who sees something very clearly, but not in its relations, and it is so in the attempts to solve phases of the labor problem. One man sees a thing very clearly; he sees that the temperance question involves the happiness and economic conditions of men, and he thinks that if temperance principles could only prevail the world would be happy. Another man ignores that and says, 'If you can only establish industrial arbitration you will settle all your difficulties.' Another man thinks that the eight-hour day would solve the problem and remove all difficulties attending industrial conditions. All these things are good, but they must be considered together in their relations one to the other, or else you are simply setting up bricks to be knocked down. Our duty, then, whether as Commissioners of Labor, or in whatever capacity we may serve, is to help contribute to the sum of knowledge which shall ultimately soften this struggle without attempting to remove that divine discontent which makes the world what it is, and which gives us whatever civilization now exists."

The work of securing the desired statistical information has been somewhat difficult, principally due to a fear on the part of many of the unions that the facts elicited would be used to their detriment. Accompanying the information blank and the letter requesting that it be filled out, was the following circular letter, which was sent to all the unions in the State the addresses of which could be ascertained, and which greatly aided the Bureau in securing information that otherwise would have been withheld :

"HARTFORD, Conn., April 1, 1898.

To Organized Labor of Connecticut:

"FELLOW WORKERS:—Your attention is respectfully called to the accompanying blank form, issued by the Commissioner of Labor Statistics, and his letter requesting your organization to have the same filled and returned to him. Grouped in totals, by trades and localities, these facts will be disseminated by the Bureau, and will prove of inestimable value to our cause. It is plain to all of us that hitherto the lack of statistical information of this character placed Organized Labor at a great disadvantage when it had under consideration matters pertaining to wages and hours. Members of a trade in one part of the State should always know the exact economic status of their fellow craftsmen in other sections so that they may act intelligently on subjects affecting their welfare. The diffusion of knowledge concerning the income of the workers, the number unemployed and the causes of idleness at stated periods would unquestionably lead to a universal discussion of the subject, and bring about a reformation of the social system that would eventually provide permanent employment for the toilers at living wages and reduced daily working time. Moreover, the public generally, and business men particularly, will be more apt to heed the reasonable demands of the Unions if they have at their command official statistics proving the justness of their claims.

"Much more could be written in favor of the Commissioner's plan, but we believe that sufficient has been said to show that labor's interests will be advanced materially if the organizations will promptly send him the required statistics.

"We, therefore, strongly urge every member of your organization to take a personal interest in this matter and co-operate with the Commissioner of Labor Statistics in his efforts in labor's behalf. We heartily commend his work in this direction, and trust it will be a complete success.

"Fraternally yours,

"ELI BRUNELL,

"Prest. Conn. State Branch A. F. of L.

"J. D. COWPER,

"State Organizer."

THE QUESTIONS ASKED TO WHICH ANSWERS WERE DESIRED WERE:

(1) Name of organization.

(2) Date of organization.

(3) Number of men, Women, when organized.

(4) Number of men, Women, at present time.

(5) Trade wages (per day): Highest, $ Lowest, $ Average, $

(6) What benefits are provided?

(7) Hours of labor (weekly), On Saturday.

(8) How many weeks in the year can members usually obtain employment?

(9) Have wages been increased or decreased as a result of organization?

(10) If increased, was it voluntary, by demand or by strike?

(11) Have hours of labor been increased or decreased as a result of organization?

(12) Do you favor shorter hours with a proportionate reduction of pay?

(13) Has your Union engaged in any strikes? If so, for what object? Was it successful or unsuccessful?

(14) How many of the members of your Union are employed?

(15) How many of the members of your Union are unemployed?

(16) What is your estimate as to the number of your trade that is unorganized in your locality?

(17) How do the wages paid organized and unorganized labor in your trade compare?

(18) Has organization been of benefit to your trade?

(19) Suggest anything that will improve the condition of the craft.

The answers given to Question No. 3 were so unsatisfactory, owing to loss of their records by several of the unions, that no attempt has been made to collate them.

Question No. 12 was answered in the negative by all save seven unions. A barber's union states that the same amount of work could be done in a shorter time, and would not call for a reduction of pay. Only six unions gave an affirmative answer. The others want shorter hours and the same pay.

The answers given to Question No. 10 were so largely "guesswork" that the tabulation has been omitted.

In answer to Question No. 17 it was stated by nearly all that wages had been increased from 15 to 35 per cent. as a result of organization, and by the others that organization had prevented the reduction of wages. As to the general benefits that have been secured by organization, the information is best given under the heading "Notes from the Unions." Answers were received, in all, from 105 unions.

In addition to the unions, from which replies were received, there are 34 from which it has been impossible to get any return whatever. Requests were made two, three and in some cases, four times, but the request was repeatedly ignored, notwithstanding the fact that stamped envelopes were enclosed for reply.

The location and names of the unions, failing to make reply, follow:

ANSONIA.—
Buffers and Polishers.

BRIDGEPORT.—
Bricklayers and Plasterers.
Engineers.
Elastic Goring Weavers.
Granite Cutters.
Suspender Weavers.

BRISTOL.—
Buffers and Polishers.

DANBURY.—
Engineers.

DERBY.—
Plumbers and Gas Fitters.

HARTFORD.—
Core Makers.
Cornice Makers.
Horseshoers.
Locomotive Firemen.

HARTFORD.—*Continued.*

Machine Woodworkers.
Painters.
Rubber Goods Workers.
Screwmakers.
Stone Cutters.
Stone Masons.
Stone Tenders.
Tailors.

MERIDEN.—

Iron Moulders.
Granite Workers.

NAUGATUCK.—

Iron Moulders.

NEW HAVEN.—

Brewers.
Buffers and Polishers.
Stereotypers.

NORWICH.—

Bricklayers and Plasterers.

SHELTON.—

Knife Grinders.

WALLINGFORD.—

Buffers and Polishers.

WATERBURY.—

Brewers.
Carpenters.
Iron Moulders.

In nearly every instance the blanks were returned correctly and intelligently filled out. An invitation was extended to the unions to state what, in their opinion, would benefit the condition of the several organized crafts, and the great majority of them made use of the opportunity thus afforded. With but few and slight alterations, the answers are given as received, under the heading "Notes from the Unions." Two replies which were redolent with anarchy have not been used, as it is not the work of this Bureau to disseminate economic theories, foreign in their origin, unsuited to our labor conditions, and opposed by the vast majority of the intelligent workmen of the State. That these workmen are intelligent, no one will question after reading the matter given under the caption above referred to.

An analysis of the figures shows that of the one hundred and five unions reporting, forty-nine have been organized during or since 1890. Further analysis shows that organization has been of immense benefit to the men directly interested, and also to the general public by the avoidance of strikes and the general disorder which follow them.

In this State it cannot be claimed by any one that the uniting together of men of the various crafts is for the purpose of antagonizing the manufacturers of the State. On the contrary, it is asserted that never has there been a better understanding between the men employed in the shops and mills in Connecticut and the employers than exists at the present time. Union men recognize, as never before, the fact that one manufacturer cannot pay high wages and run his mill a reasonable number of hours in competition with his fellow-manufacturer in the same line of goods who pay low wages and keeps his power going for an unlimited time.

In view of this fact, organized labor, not only in Connecticut but all over the country, is concentrating its efforts to secure uniform laws concerning hours of labor, and by thorough co-operation a uniform rate of wages. During the year past a number of unions have been formed among the textile workers. To them this question of hours and wages is of vital importance. In the South, as is shown in another chapter of this report, low wages and long hours are the prevailing rule. A cotton mill owner, interested in four mills in this State, stated to an officer of this Bureau that they had no desire to reduce wages or increase the hours of labor to meet this competition and that they were in complete harmony with the efforts of organized labor to secure national legislation tending to equalize conditions.

Thus far, organized labor in Connecticut has shown itself to be a conservative and self-respecting body. The rules and regulations governing most of the unions make it impossible for one or two men to precipitate a strike. Before one is ordered every possible means must be used to effect a settlement of any question which may be in dispute between employer and employe. That these unions are acting up to this principle is evidenced by the fact that in the whole history of the one hundred and five unions represented in this report but twelve strikes have occurred. The record covers a period extending from 1850 to the present time. It is to be understood that these figures do not refer to unorganized trades. The investigation further shows that, since one of a similar character made in 1891 (see Seventh Annual Report), the number of unions and their membership has been largely increased.

The deductions that may fairly be drawn as a direct result of this investigation clearly indicate that trades unionism in the State is, in general, in a healthy and prosperous condition, that it aims primarily to ameliorate the condition of the employe and not to antagonize the employer, that its needs and shortcomings are known and understood, and that intelligent and continual effort is being put forth to improve the standing and efficiency of all organized craftsmen. The letter from the locomotive engineers demonstrates what may be accomplished by a thorough understanding between employer and employe, and the general plea for an efficient apprentice law indicates a praiseworthy regard for the future well-being of the Connecticut laborer.

NATIONAL ORGANIZATIONS REPRESENTED IN CONNECTICUT.

Amalgamated Woodworkers Association.
American Federation of Labor.
Brewery Workers.
Bricklayers and Plasterers International Union.
Brotherhood of Bookbinders.
Brotherhood of Locomotive Engineers.
Brotherhood of Locomotive Firemen.
Brotherhood of Painters and Decorators.
Brotherhood of Railway Trainmen.
Elastic Goring Weavers Amalgamated Association.
International Association of Machinists.
International Brotherhood of Brass Workers.
International Cigarmakers Union.
International Typographical Union.
Iron Moulders Union of North America.
Journeymen Bakers and Confectioners International Union.
Journeymen Barbers International Union.
Journeymen Horseshoers National Union.
Journeymen Tailors Union of America.
Knights of Labor and Industry.
Metal Polishers and Buffers International Union.
Musicians Protective Association.
National Association of Fur Hat Makers.
National Association of Hat Finishers.
National Association of Stationary Engineers.
National Beamer Tenders Association.
National Brotherhood of Electrical Workers.
National Cotton Weavers Union.
National Loom Fixers Association.
National Mule Spinners Association.
National Silk Workers Association.
National Union of Stone Masons.
Printing Pressmen Union.
United Association of Journeymen Plumbers.
United Brotherhood of Carpenters and Joiners.
United Hatters of North America.

AMERICAN FEDERATION OF LABOR.

The Connecticut Branch of the American Federation of Labor was formed in Hartford in 1887, mainly through the efforts of the Central Labor Union of Hartford. Representatives were present from thirty-five local and central bodies. The trades represented were :

Bakers,
Barbers,
Boxmakers,
Bricklayers,
Carpenters and Joiners,
Cigarmakers,
Clerks,
Horseshoers,
Hatters,
Hodcarriers,
Iron Moulders,
Masons' Tenders,
Printers,
Tailors,
Woodcarvers.

At its first meeting it declared its objects to be:

"I. To assist in establishing National and International Trades Unions, based upon a strict recognition of the autonomy of each trade, and the promotion and advancement of such bodies.

"II. The encouragement and formation of local Trade and Labor Unions in every city and town in this State, and the combination of these bodies into a State Federation of Trade and Labor Unions, to assist and aid each other.

"III. To secure State legislation in the interests of the working people, and to influence public opinion by peaceful and legal methods in favor of organized labor.

"IV. To aid and encourage the labor press of our State, and to establish an organ of the State Federation as soon as deemed advisable."

This organization holds a convention each year in some place designated by the preceding convention. It has had an active growth, having at the present time affiliated with it eighty unions and central bodies. The number of members represented by the affiliated unions is stated to be 5,000.

The basis of representation is that—

"Each Union having one hundred members or less shall be entitled to one delegate, and one additional delegate for each additional hundred members or majority fraction thereof. Each central body shall be entitled to but one delegate."

Since 1896 a State organizer has been kept in the field organizing new unions and visiting the weaker ones. He reports that during this present year twenty-four (24) new unions have been formed, with a membership of fourteen hundred and forty-four (1,444).

CENTRAL LABOR UNIONS.

These organizations, of which there are eight in the State, are composed of representatives from the local unions situated in their immediate vicinity. Their object is the same as that of the State Branch. These organizations are located in—

Bridgeport,	New Britain,
Danbury,	New Haven,
Hartford,	Norwich,
Meriden,	South Norwalk.

JOURNEYMEN BAKERS AND CONFECTIONERS INTERNATIONAL UNION OF AMERICA.

The Journeymen Bakers and Confectioners International Union of America was organized January 13, 1886, at Pittsburg, Pa.

"OBJECT OF THE ORGANIZATION.

"The Union aims at the promotion of the material and intellectual welfare of all workmen in the baking trade: (1) By organization; (2) by education; (3) by the reduction of the hours of labor; (4) by gradually abolishing such evils as may prevail in the baking trade; (5) by establishing labor bureaus wherever possible; (6) by assisting members in legal causes in matters concerning the Union; (7) by agitating the abolition of nightwork, and by using its influence with the lawmakers of each State to secure the passage of Sanitary Bake-shop Laws.

"MEMBERSHIP—DUTIES AND RIGHTS.

"No person shall become a member of this organization until he has worked at least three years at some branch of the trade. After that period he may become a member on the recommendation of a member of this organization. No distinction shall be made on account of race, sex, creed or nationality.

"STRIKES.

"Section 1. In case of difficulties between employes and employers, it becomes the duty of the Local Union to prevent strikes as much as possible by attempting to settle such difficulties in a peaceful way. Only in the event that all attempts at a peaceful settlement shall prove of no avail, or if the demands of the employers should be beneath the dignity of the employes and contrary to the principles of a Unionist, a strike shall be resorted to.

"Section 2. Should a strike in one locality seem unavoidable, then it shall be attempted to limit such strikes to as few shops as possible, so as to enable those remaining at work to support their fellow-members on strike.

"Section 4. Strikes can only be declared when three-fourths of the members in good standing vote in favor thereof. The same vote is required to declare a strike ended.

"Section 5. No member shall receive a strike benefit in the first week of a strike.

"Section 6. If a Local Union proposes to go on a strike subject to being aided by the International Union, such Union must make an application to the Executive Board before going on strike, wherein all the reasons must be stated that lead to that strike, together with a statement of the attempts that were made to accomplish a peaceful settlement of the difficulties; also a statement as to how many members may eventually become involved in such a strike.

"Section 8. No strikes shall be decided upon unless every member has been invited in writing, or personally, by an officer of the Union to attend the meeting where it is to be acted upon."

A sick benefit of five dollars per week and a death benefit of one hundred dollars is paid to members in good standing.

BROTHERHOOD OF CARPENTERS AND JOINERS.

The National Brotherhood of Carpenters and Joiners was organized in Chicago, Ill., April, 1881. Several attempts had been made previous to that time, but the unions formed were not of long duration, owing largely to lack of concerted action. Its jurisdiction extends over all the States of the Union. The society is governed by an executive board of five members, elected by the local unions within ten miles of the city selected as headquarters. The qualifications for membership are that the applicant must be a carpenter and joiner, engaged at wood-work, and competent to command average wages, not more than sixty years of age, of good moral character and sound health, and not afflicted with any disease or subject to any complaint likely to endanger life. Any stairbuilder, millwright, planing mill hand or any cabinet-maker, engaged at carpenter work, or any carpenter running woodworking machinery, is eligible to membership, if possessed of the above qualifications.

Any member who engages in the sale of intoxicating liquors must withdraw from the organization.

At the beginning, the object was purely protective in its character, upholding wages, struggling to advance them, and to shorten the hours of labor. At the National Convention, held in Philadelphia in 1882, it laid down the settled policy of advocating the adoption of nine hours as a day's work. That is the rule now prevailing in Connecticut. The policy of the order is to avoid strikes and to render them almost impossible. To order a strike requires a two-thirds vote by secret ballot of the members, and all members must have two weeks' notice to attend the meeting. Then the consent of the General Executive Board must be obtained, and, if granted, the "Protective Fund" of the entire Brotherhood is at the command of the local union in trouble. But before the union takes a ballot on the subject, an arbitration committee from the union must wait on the employers and endeavor to adjust the difficulty. Members in good standing are entitled to the following benefits: Member's death, $200.00; funeral of wife, $50.00; for total disability by accident while at work, $200.00; sickness, $3.00 per week.

The order has a membership of over fifty thousand.

CIGARMAKERS INTERNATIONAL UNION OF AMERICA.

The Cigarmakers International Union was organized in New York City on June 21, 1864, by twenty-three persons as delegates from several local unions. Previous to this time efforts to organize had been of a local or State character, and had met with varying success.

The more active and wisest among the craft foresaw that no lasting results could be obtained unless the fragmentary elements composing the scattered local bodies could be bound together in one compact organization. Step by step, and by dint of perseverance and self-sacrifice, it has now reached a membership of thirty-two thousand, and has a very large reserve fund to draw upon in aiding its members.

The principal objects of the order are declared to be—

"The sustenance of the unfortunate and distressed among our members; the promotion and protection of our social, economic and political interests, and the advancement of education upon those subjects, a broad and intelligent conception of which is most necessary to a true solution of the labor problem and the final emancipation of the wage-worker."

The Bureau is indebted to Mr. G. W. Perkins, President of the International Union, for the following facts:

The initiation fee is $3, and the weekly dues are 30 cents.

It pays the following benefits: $5 per week in case of strike; $3 per week out-of-work benefit; $5 per week sick benefit; traveling loan benefit; death benefit from $50 to $550, and a wife and widowed mother funeral benefit of $40.

In the past eighteen years it has expended, all told, in benefits, the munificent sum of $3,718,686.38.

The following table presents the total benefits paid for the last eighteen years and two months:

BENEFITS PAID IN EIGHTEEN YEARS AND TWO MONTHS.

Year.	Strike benefit.	Sick benefit.	Death benefit.	Traveling benefit.	Out-of-work benefit.
1879	$3,668.23	....	....	....	....
1880	4,950.36	....	....	$2,808.15	....
1881	21,797.68	$3,987.78	$75.00	12,747.09	....
1882	44,850.41	17,145.29	1,674.25	20,386.64	....
1883	27,812.13	22,250.56	2,690.00	37,135.20	....
1884	143,547.36	31,551.50	3,920.00	39,632.08	....
1885	61,087.28	29,379.89	4,214.00	26,683.54	....
1886	54,402.61	42,225.59	4,820.00	31,835.71	....
1887	13,871.62	63,900.88	8,850.00	49,281.04	....
1888	45,303.62	58,824.19	21,319.75	42,894.75	....
1889	5,202.52	59,519.94	19,175.50	43,540.44	....
1890	18,414.27	64,660.47	26,043.00	37,914.72	$22,760.50
1891	33,531.78	87,472.97	38,068.35	58,535.73	21,223.50
1892	37,477.60	89,906.30	44,701.97	47,732.47	17,460.75
1893	18,228.15	104,391.83	49,458.33	60,475.11	89,402.75
1894	44,966.76	106,758.37	62,158.77	42,154.17	174,517.25
1895	44,039.06	112,567.06	66,725.98	41,657.16	166,377.25
1896	27,446.46	109,208.62	78,768.09	33,076.22	175,767.25
1897	12,175.09	112,774.63	69,186.67	29,067.04	117,471.40
Total	$662,772.99	$1,116,525.82	$501,849.66	$652,557.26	$784,980.65

Total benefits paid in 1896 .... $424,266.64
Total benefits paid in 1897 .... 340,674.83
Grand total of benefits paid 3,718,686.38

In addition to these benefits it has succeeded in raising the wages of its members from 20 to 50 per cent., and in shortening the hours of labor to eight per day. The eight-hour day has been in operation since May 1, 1886, being inaugurated and gained independent of any other craft at the time.

The successful achievements of the International Union are so many and varied, that space will not permit me to give even a synopsis of them. However, chief among them was the adoption of an admirable financial system and the payment of high dues; the shortening of the hours of labor; the adoption of a splendid chain of benefits and the adoption of the "Blue Label."

The payment of high dues is considered one of the most potent factors that has led up to our present success, as it has allowed the accumulation of a large reserve fund, which is largely responsible for our success, and thereby enabled us to not only keep our membership intact, but to increase its numerical strength.

It is a fact that since this fund assumed fair proportions, we have succeeded in raising wages in a large number of instances without strike or any expense to the International Union. Employers hesitate in the face of such formidable weapons to bring on a contest, and in recent years, as a rule, when our demands have been tempered with justice, they have been readily acceded to.

We gained more advances with our present fund and expended less money for strike benefit with our 36,000 members, than we did in former years with 12,000 members. In other words, more strike benefit was paid when we had only 12,000 members and a small defense fund than we expend now with about 36,000 members and a large defense fund, and still the percentage of increases in wages is greater now than at the former period.

During the unprecedented industrial and commercial depression now drawing to a close, we have expended thousands of dollars to our unfortunate members out of employment, which to say the least, enabled them to retain their standing and claim on benefits.

The order has a membership of 757 in Connecticut, among whom are three women, distributed among eleven local unions.

THE BROTHERHOOD OF LOCOMOTIVE ENGINEERS.

In April, 1863, a few engineers in the employ of the Michigan Central Railroad Company conceived the idea of forming an association to promote the welfare and interest of their profession and elevate their standing and character as men. With these objects in view, they assembled at the house of one of their number, in the city of Marshall, Mich. The result of their deliberation was the issuing of an invitation to the engineers employed on the adjacent roads to meet in the city of Detroit on the fifth day of May. In response to the invitation, at the appointed time, ten delegates assembled, who, with but little formality in their organization, entered upon their duties, and, with the assistance of a few engineers residing in Detroit, a constitution and by-laws were presented and adopted, embodying the fundamental principles of the present organization.

The necessity of something further on the part of engineers than the common consent to become and remain members of the association so long as suited their own convenience became apparent to the minds of the delegates, and an obligation, as a bond of union, was formulated and unanimously adopted, and on the 8th day of May, 1863, twelve engineers joined hands and hearts, pledging themselves to support the constitution and by-laws, assist the needy and maintain the right.

Officers were elected, and Detroit Division No. 1, Brotherhood of the Footboard, stood forth as the pioneer in the great work of reformation and elevation of the locomotive engineers of this continent.

During the first year of its existence, forty-four sub-divisions were organized. On the 17th of August, 1864, the first convention was held in the city of Indianapolis, Ind., with forty-four division representatives, at which time the name and title of the organization was changed to its present one, making it international in character, so that all locomotive engineers, regardless of nationality, would be eligible.

The organization has been in existence, as a society, thirty-five years, and during that time has gradually increased in numbers and importance; emerging almost silently from its original obscurity. At the present time the Brotherhood has a membership of 32,000, distributed among 538 divisions, three divisions are located in Connecticut with a membership of 378. Their membership contains nine-tenths of the best locomotive engineers on this continent; and they have gained an enviable position by a strict adherence to their mottoes: "Sobriety, Truth, Justice and Morality," "Vigilance, not Violence," and "Do unto others as ye would that they should do unto you, and so fulfil the law." They stand aloof from all political bodies and sects and ignore all questions of creed and race, and look only to the improvement and protection of the locomotive engineers and their families.

At the convention held in the city of Boston in November, 1866, the publication of a monthly journal, to be devoted exclusively to the interests of the profession, was authorized and the first number was issued in January, 1867, composed of 16 pages; it now has 112 pages and has at the present time a circulation of nearly 37,000, including among its subscribers residents of Europe and India. It contains a list of all subdivisions, together with the names of the officers and where they are located.

On the 3rd of December, 1867, there was established an insurance association, which pays to the heirs of deceased members, or to a member who is unfortunate enough to lose a hand, arm, limb, or eyesight, the full amount of the policy or policies held. Policies are for $1,500, and a member may carry one, two or three, making $1,500, $3,000 or $4,500. The cost of carrying one policy of $1,500 is from 23 to 25 dollars a year. In the aggregate, the sum of $5,771,214.61 has been paid to injured brothers and heirs of deceased members, besides disbursing, out of their hard earnings, thirty-five to forty thousand dollars among the widows, orphans and needy of the order at every convention.

A large number of the divisions have a weekly indemnity insurance, each having their own law, which vary in the amount of dues and indemnity. The weekly indemnity is usually about twelve dollars.

The organization has contracts with 107 railroad companies, which include nearly all the great trunk lines. These contracts embody rates of pay and rules and regulations governing overtime, treatment of the employes and for the prevention of unjust discharge or suspension.

Through the instrumentality of this organized effort, the remuneration for services has been greatly increased, overtime allowance properly adjusted, and the character of those who comprise it elevated and educated, and peace and harmony maintained between the employer and employe.

(EXTRACTS FROM CONSTITUTION.)

"SECTION 1. This organization shall be known under the name and title of the 'GRAND INTERNATIONAL BROTHERHOOD OF LOCOMOTIVE ENGINEERS,' and its purpose shall be to more effectually combine the interests of locomotive engineers, to elevate their standing as such, and their character as men. * * * * * No person shall become a member of the Brotherhood unless he is a white man 21 years of age, and can read and write, and is a man of good moral character, temperate habits, and a locomotive engineer in good standing, and in actual service as a locomotive engineer when proposed, and has had experience as such at least one year, each Division to be the judge of what constitutes one year's experience. * * * * * No member of this organization shall be allowed to join any other labor organization, under penalty of expulsion by his Division. * * * * * The influence or sympathy of the Brotherhood, as a body, shall never be enlisted or used in favor of any political or religous organization whatever; no member of this brotherhood shall be permitted to discuss in any manner in Division, or while discussing Division matters, any religious matter, or criticise the religious belief of any member, and any Division permitting the same to be done shall have their charter suspended, and all members participating in such discussion shall be expelled."

IRON MOULDERS UNION OF NORTH AMERICA.

The iron moulders had local organizations early in the century. In Cincinnati they were sufficiently organized in 1849 to maintain a strike that lasted for nine months, and in which they were eventually successful. On July 5, 1859, the various local unions came together and formed the Iron Moulders Union of North America. The constitution of the union provides the following stringent regulations for the government of strikes:

"Any subordinate union requiring the assistance of this union to vindicate its rights and privileges under this constitution, shall be required to conform to the following sections, and shall await an official answer.

"When a difficulty occurs under the jurisdiction of any local union through a reduction of wages or through the principles of our organization being jeopardized in any manner, the union under whose jurisdiction the trouble exists shall hold a meeting at once to consider the same. If, in its judgment, the matter is worthy the attention of the executive officer, it shall lay the case before him. The president shall then, either by deputy or in person, proceed to the place at once and make a thorough examination as to the facts in the case. He shall do his utmost to settle the trouble amicably between employers and employed. Failing to adjust the difficulty, he shall lay the matter before the executive board immediately, which board, in conjunction with the president, shall have absolute control of all strikes and lockouts. They shall see that no more strikes are on hand at any one time than the organization is able to handle. They shall concentrate the whole prestige and force of the National Union, financially and otherwise, in the direction most needed. It shall be considered sufficient cause for expulsion from the National Union should any local union attempt to assume responsibility of striking without their grievance being considered by the president and having the sanction of the executive board before going out."

Since 1880 it has paid a death benefit of $100 to the families of all members in good standing at death. Over fifteen per cent. of its income has been thus expended.

MUSICIANS PROTECTIVE UNION.

The Musicians Protective Union, while not strictly a labor organization, can properly be classed as such, as the object of the union is declared to be "To unite the instrumental portion of the musical profession for the better protection of its interests in general, the establishment of a minimum rate of prices to be charged by the members of said union for their professional services, and the enforcement of good faith and fair dealing between its members."

Any musician of good moral standing, who takes an engagement for money, is eligible to membership.

No member of the union is allowed to play with a resident non-union member, but may play with any musician living out of the town where the union is located, provided, always, that the scale of prices adopted by the union is adhered to.

"Until all indebtedness for musical services rendered by any member of the union, to any society, organization, or individual, shall have been satisfactorily settled for, all members shall be restricted from taking or filling any engagement with the society, organization or individual." A scale of prices is fixed by each local union covering nearly every form of service likely to be called for.

INTERNATIONAL TYPOGRAPHICAL UNION.

The organized printers have existed as an "International" body since 1869. In 1852 they were known as the National Union, but the title was changed in 1869 in order to admit the members of the craft residing in Canada. A National convention of printers met in New York in 1850 and in Baltimore in 1851, but little progress was made toward a permanent organization. At the convention held in 1852 the National Typographical Union was formed. From that time the organization has grown in strength and power.

The International Union regards strikes as inexpedient and to be deprecated, except where principles and rules of the order have been violated. Recognizing strikes as detrimental to the best interests of the craft, it directs subordinate unions not to order a strike until every possible effort has been made to settle the difficulty by arbitration.

In case it shall be considered by a subordinate union that a strike is necessary, the consent of the "National Executive Council" of the order must first be obtained.

The constitution provides as follows:

"An Executive Council, consisting of the president of the International Typographical Union, the chief organizer and a vice-president or state deputy, shall be convened, when necessary, by the president of the International Typographical Union. It shall be the duty of the Executive Council to consider all appeals for aid for strikes or lockouts from subordinate unions, to investigate such matters, and it shall decide in all cases. When a strike has been approved by the Executive Council it shall notify the subordinate union, and, in its discretion, order an assessment of from two to twenty-five cents per capita to be paid to the subordinate union making the appeal. Any union inaugurating a strike, without the approval of the Executive Council, shall receive no benefit on account of the strike from the strike fund; *provided*, that where a union strikes in case of emergency, without consent as above, they shall be entitled to all benefits if the strike be subsequently approved by the Executive Council."

A funeral benefit of $60 is paid by the International Union. Sick benefits are paid by the local unions.

"OBJECTS OF THE ORGANIZATION.

"Section 2. The objects of this Union shall be the maintenance of a fair rate of wages, the encouragement of good workmen and the exposition and prevention of all subterfuge whatever by persons employed in the printing business, as journeymen, in working under any arrangement whereby less than the established rates are paid; to endeavor to replace strikes by arbitration and conciliation in the settlement of all disputes concerning wages and conditions of employment, and also to relieve the deserving needy and provide for the burial of deceased members."

At the quadrennial meeting of the National Body, held in Denver, Colorado, in 1894, it was decided that the time had now come when a demand should be made for a nine-hour workday, and a committee, styled "Shorter Workday Committee," was appointed to make preparations for such a demand. The question had been discussed and approved in every subordinate branch of the order since that time, and it was decided that the time had come when the demand should be made. The committees of the allied printing trades met with the committee of the United Typothetæ, an association of employing printers, at Syracuse, New York, October 10th, and asked that an agreement might be made to establish nine hours as a day's work. The subject was discussed for several days, and a compromise was effected whereby a nine-and-one-half-hour day should be given after November 21st, 1898, and a nine-hour day after November, 1899. These conditions were agreed to by the Connecticut Branch of the Typothetæ at a meeting held in New Haven in October.

The arrangement is now in effect in all the leading printing establishments in this State, beginning November 21, 1898.

SICK AND DEATH BENEFITS PAID.

Bakers.—
For sickness, $5.00 per week, not exceeding 26 weeks.
For death, $50.00 to $100.

Barbers.—
For sickness, $5.00 per week, not exceeding 13 weeks.
Death, $50.

Bricklayers and Plasterers.—
$5.00 per week for sickness or disability.

Buffers and Polishers.—
$5.00 per week during a strike.

Carpenters and Joiners.—
Wife's funeral, $50.
Disability of member, $100 to $400.
Member's death, $300.

Cigarmakers.—
In case of strike, $5.00 per week.
Out of work, $3.00 per week.
Sickness, $5.00 per week.
Death of member, $50 to $500.
Wife or widowed mother's funeral, $40.

Cotton Weavers.—
$5.00 per week while on strike

Drivers Protective Association.—
Sickness, $5.00.
Death, $50.

Elastic Goring Weavers.—
Death benefit, $100.

Hatmakers.—
Burial benefit, $100.

Hat Trimmers.—
Burial benefit, $300.

Horse Nail Workers.—
Sickness, $5.00 per week.
Death, $50.

Horseshoers.—
$5.00 per week for sickness, not exceeding 10 weeks.

Loom Fixers.—
Weekly benefit during strike or shut down.

Machinists.—
Sickness, $5.00 per week.
Death, $50.

Mule Spinners.—
$5.00 while on strike.

Printing Pressmen.—
Death benefit, $250.

Railway Trainmen.—
Insurance, death or loss of limb, $1,200.

Tailors.—
Sickness, $5.00 per week.
During strike, $6.00.
Death, $100.

RATES OF WAGES AND HOURS OF LABOR OF ORGANIZED LABOR.

BAKERS AND CONFECTIONERS.

Town.	Name of organization.	Organized.	Wages per day. Highest.	Wages per day. Lowest.	Wages per day. Average.	Hours of labor Weekly.	Hours of labor Saturday.	Average number weeks employed.
			$	$	$			
New Haven...	Bakers Union No. 11............	1886	3.00	2.00	2.50	72	14	52
Hartford......	Bakers Union No. 8.............	1886	2.50	1.70	2.25	72	13	52
Bridgeport....	Bakers Union No. 38............	1886	3.25	1.25	2.25	90	19	52
Meriden.......	Bakers Union No.	1891	2.66	2.00	2.25	73	13	52
New Britain...	Bakers Union No. 107...........	1892	2.65	1.65	2.15	68	13	52
Danbury......	Bakers Union No. 193...........	1897	3.00	1.75	2.25	60	12	52

JOURNEYMEN BARBERS.

Danbury......	Barbers Union No. 175..........	1895	2.25	2.00	2.00	74	14	52
Meriden.......	Barbers Union No. 88...........	1896	2.33	1.67	2.00	61	17	52
Norwich.......	Barbers Union No.	1897	2.50	1.65	2.00	74	14	52
New London..	Barbers Union No. 136..........	1898	......	......	......	73	15¼	52

BOOKBINDERS.

Hartford......	Bookbinders......................	1892	3.25	2.25	2.75	59	9	50

BRASS MOULDERS.

Meriden.......	Brass Moulders.................	1886	3.00	2.25	2.50	54	9	40

RATES OF WAGES AND HOURS OF LABOR OF ORGANIZED LABOR —*Continued.*

BREWERY WORKERS.

Town.	Name of organization.	Organized.	Wages per day.			Hours of labor		Average number weeks employed.
			Highest.	Lowest.	Average.	Weekly.	Saturday.	
			$	$	$			
Hartford......	Brewers Union No.	1887	2.60	2.50	2.50	60	10	52
Meriden.......	Brewers Union No.	1895	3.33	2.00	2.50	60	10	52
Waterbury....	Brewers Union No.	1897	2.60	2.50	2.50	60	10	52

BRICKLAYERS AND PLASTERERS.

Hartford......	Bricklayers and Plasterers No. 1	1885	4.00	3.50	3.75	54	9	40

BUFFERS AND POLISHERS.

Meriden.......	Buffers and Polishers No. 48....	1886	3.00	2.00	2.50	54	9	40
Waterbury....	Buffers and Polishers No.	1895	2.50	1.75	2.25	60	10	40
Bridgeport....	Buffers and Polishers No.	1896	3.50	1.25	2.00	59	9	40
Middletown...	Buffers and Polishers No.	1897	2.50	1.75	2.50	59	9	36

CARPENTERS AND JOINERS.

Hartford......	Carpenters and Joiners No. 43..	1882	3.00	2.00	2.50	54	9	45
New Britain ..	Carpenters and Joiners No. 97..	1885	2.75	1.75	2.25	54	9	40
Bridgeport....	Carpenters and Joiners No. 115.	1885	2.50	1.50	2.00	54	9	40
Norwich......	Carpenters and Joiners No. 137.	1886	2.50	1.75	2.00	54	9	40
Norwalk	Carpenters and Joiners No. 746.	1891	2.50	2.00	2.25	54	9	50
New Haven...	Carpenters and Joiners No. 79..	1892	3.00	1.50	2.00	54	9	40
Stamford......	Carpenters and Joiners No. 210.	1897	2.88	1.75	2.50	53	8	45
Shelton........	Carpenters and Joiners No 127.	1898	2.75	1.75	2.50	60	10	40
Meriden.......	Carpenters and Joiners No.	1885	3.00	1.25	2.50	54	9	42

RATES OF WAGES AND HOURS OF LABOR OF ORGANIZED LABOR—*Continued.*

CIGARMAKERS INTERNATIONAL UNION.

Town.	Name of organization.	Organized.	Wages per day. Highest.	Lowest.	Average.	Hours of labor Weekly.	Saturday.	Average number weeks employed.
			$	$	$			
New Haven...	Cigarmakers Union No. 39......	1871	3.75	1.50	2.00	48	8	44
Hartford......	Cigarmakers Union No. 42......	1880	3.60	1.50	2.25	48	8	48
Long Hill......	Cigarmakers Union No. 139.....	1881	3.00	2.00	2.50	44	4	45
So. Norwalk..	Cigarmakers Union No.	1880	3.00	1.50	1.75	48	8	50
Danbury......	Cigarmakers Union No. 180.....	1882	2.50	1.50	1.75	46	6	36
Suffield........	Cigarmakers Union No. 156.....	1883	3.50	1.50	2.50	48	8	48
Bridgeport....	Cigarmakers Union No. 282.....	1886	2.50	1.50	2.00	48	8	40
Ansonia.......	Cigarmakers Union No. 103.....	1884	2.50	......	......	48	8	50
New London..	Cigarmakers Union No. 189.....	1893	2.00	1.50	1.75	48	8	50
Waterbury....	Cigarmakers Union No. 395.....	1897	2.50	1.50	1.70	46	6	46
Norwich.......	Cigarmakers Union No. 407.....	1898	3.00	1.50	2.00	48	8	52

DRIVERS PROTECTIVE UNION.

Hartford......	Drivers Protective Union.......	1895	2.50	1.50	1.75	60	10	52

ELECTRICAL WORKERS UNION.

Hartford......	Electrical Workers..............	1897	2.50	2.50	2.50	60	10	40

ENGINEERS, LOCOMOTIVE.

New Haven...	Brotherhood Locomotive Eng'rs	1866	4.50	2.00	3.50	8	8	52
Hartford......	Brotherhood Locomotive Eng'rs	1883	4.00	3.00	3.50	8	8	52
New London..	Brotherhood Locomotive Eng'rs	1888	3.50	2.50	2.75	8	8	52

RATES OF WAGES AND HOURS OF LABOR OF ORGANIZED LABOR—*Continued.*

ENGINEERS, STATIONARY.

Town.	Name of organization.	Organized.	Wages per day. Highest.	Wages per day. Lowest.	Wages per day. Average.	Hours of labor. Weekly.	Hours of labor. Saturday.	Average number weeks employed.
Meriden.......	Stationary Engineers...........	1883	$ 4.50	$ 2.50	$ 3.00	....	....	52

HATTERS UNIONS.

Town.	Name of organization.	Organized.	Highest.	Lowest.	Average.	Weekly.	Saturday.	Average number weeks employed.
Danbury......	Hatters Assembly, K. of L., No. 4236.....................	1885	......	......	......	60	8	30
"	Hatters Assembly, K. of L., No. 7923.....................	1886	......	......	......	60	8	30
"	Beaver Assembly, K. of L., No. 2824.....................	1884	......	......	......	60	8	40
"	Hatmakers Union...............	1850	*.....	*.....	*.....	60	8	30
"	Hat Finishers Union............	1855	5.00	1.50	2.00	60	8	30
"	Hat Coverers and Slippers Union	1885	3.00	......	3.00	60	8	30
Norwalk	Hatmakers Union...............	1860	4.00	1.50	1.60	55	5	35
"	Hat Finishers Union...........	1860	4.50	1.50	2.50	60	10	35

HORSESHOE NAIL WORKERS.

Town.	Name of organization.	Organized.	Highest.	Lowest.	Average.	Weekly.	Saturday.	Average number weeks employed.
Hartford......	Horse Nail Workers No. 1.......	1892	3.50	1.50	1.80	59	9	50

HORSESHOERS UNION.

Town.	Name of organization.	Organized.	Highest.	Lowest.	Average.	Weekly.	Saturday.	Average number weeks employed.
New Haven...	Horseshoers Union No. 26.......	1893	3.50	2.50	2.75	59	9	45
Ansonia.......	Horseshoers Union No.	1898	3.00	2.00	2.50	60	10	52

*See notes from the unions.

RATES OF WAGES AND HOURS OF LABOR OF ORGANIZED LABOR—*Continued.*

HOUSE PAINTERS.

Town.	Name of organization.	Organized.	Wages per day. Highest.	Wages per day. Lowest.	Wages per day. Average.	Hours of labor Weekly.	Hours of labor Saturday.	Average number weeks employed.
New Britain..	House Painters Union	1890	$ 3.00	$ 2.25	$ 2.50	54	9	35

IRON MOULDERS.

Town.	Name of organization.	Organized.	Highest.	Lowest.	Average.	Weekly.	Saturday.	Average number weeks employed.
Norwalk..... .	Iron Moulders Union No. 209....	1869	4.00	2.00	2.50	60	10	45
Norwich.......	Iron Moulders Union No. 126....	......	3.00	2.00	2.50	59	9	45
Bridgeport....	Iron Moulders Union No. 110....	1879	3.00	1.80	2.25	59	9	45
Branford......	Iron Moulders Union No. 82.....	1880	2.50	2.00	2.25	60	10	50
Hartford......	Iron Moulders Union No. 72.....	1888	3.50	2.25	2.50	60	10	50
Ansonia.......	Iron Moulders Union No. 52.....	1889	3.25	2.00	2.50	60	10	45
Rocky Hill....	Iron Moulders Union No. 302....	1892	3.00	2.00	2.25	60	10	36
New Haven...	Iron Moulders Union No.	1878	2.75	1.50	2.50	54	9	50
Stamford	Iron Moulders Union No.	......	4.00	2.50	3.00	60	10	48
New Britain..	Iron Moulders Union No.	......	2.50	1.50	2.00	60	10	48

MACHINISTS AND TOOL MAKERS.

Town.	Name of organization.	Organized.	Highest.	Lowest.	Average.	Weekly.	Saturday.	Average number weeks employed.
Bridgeport....	Machinists and Tool Makers Benefit Association...........	1891	3.50	2.50	2.75	59	9	48
"	International Association of Machinists......................	......	3.25	2.00	2.75	59	9	48
Hartford......	International Association of Machinists......................	1893	3.50	2.00	2.50	59	9	52
New Britain..	International Association of Machinists......................	1894	4.00	2.00	2.75	60	10	52

RATES OF WAGES AND HOURS OF LABOR OF ORGANIZED LABOR—*Continued.*

MUSICIANS UNIONS.

Town.	Name of organization.	Organized.	Wages per day. Highest.	Lowest.	Average.	Hours of labor Weekly.	Saturday.	Average number weeks employed.
			$	$	$			
Meriden.......	Musical Protective	1889	*....	......	......	....	....	......
Hartford......	Musical Protective	1890	*....	......	......	....	....	......
Bridgeport....	Musical Protective	1896	*....	......	......	....	....	......
Danbury......	Musical Protective	1897	*....	......	......	....	....	......
Norwalk	Musical Protective	1897	*....	......	......	....	....	......

JOURNEYMEN PLUMBERS.

Town.	Name of organization.	Organized.	Highest.	Lowest.	Average.	Weekly.	Saturday.	Average number weeks employed.
Hartford......	United Association of Journeymen Plumbers................	1892	3.50	2.00	2.50	54	9	50
Meriden.......	Plumbers, Steam and Gas Fitters	1893	3.50	2.50	2.75	54	9	40
Norwich	Plumbers, Steam and Gas Fitters	1897	2.75	2.00	2.50	54	9	40
New Britain..	Plumbers, Steam and Gas Fitters	1894	3.00	2.50	2.75	54	9	52
New Haven...	Plumbers, Steam and Gas Fitters	1887	3.50	2.50	3.00	54	9	50

PRINTING PRESSMEN.

Town.	Name of organization.	Organized.	Highest.	Lowest.	Average.	Weekly.	Saturday.	Average number weeks employed.
New Haven...	Printing Pressmens Union No. 74	1896	4.25	2.50	3.50	†59	9	52
Hartford......	Printing Pressmens Union No...	1897	5.50	2.25	2.75	†59	9	52

*See notes from the unions.

† These hours apply to the job printers only. Newspaper pressmen work from six to seven hours daily.

RATES OF WAGES AND HOURS OF LABOR OF ORGANIZED LABOR — *Continued.*

RAILWAY TRAINMEN.

Town.	Name of organization.	Organized.	Wages per day. Highest.	Wages per day. Lowest.	Wages per day. Average.	Hours of labor Weekly.	Hours of labor Saturday.	Average number weeks employed.
			$	$	$			
New Haven...	Brotherhood of Railroad Trainmen...........................	1883	3.00	1.50	2.00	60	10	52
Hartford......	Brotherhood of Railroad Trainmen...........................	1885	2.25	1.95	2.00	60	10	52
Bridgeport....	Brotherhood of Railroad Trainmen...........................	1887	3.00	1.95	2.00	60	10	52
Danbury......	Brotherhood of Railroad Trainmen...........................	1889	2.75	1.90	1.95	60	10	52

SHOEMAKERS.

Danbury......	Shoemakers Union..............	1895	*.....	......	......	....	....	......

STONE MASONS.

New Haven...	Stone Masons Union............	1888	†.43	3.60	†.40	54	9	35

TAILORS.

Danbury......	Journeymen Tailors Union.....	1885	2.50	1.50	2.00	‡...	‡...	26

*See notes from unions.
†Per hour.
‡No limit.

RATES OF WAGES AND HOURS OF LABOR OF ORGANIZED LABOR—*Concluded.*

TEXTILE WORKERS.

Town.	Name of organization.	Organized.	Wages per day. Highest.	Wages per day. Lowest.	Wages per day. Average.	Hours of labor Weekly.	Hours of labor Saturday.	Average number weeks employed.
			$	$	$			
Bridgeport....	Silk Weavers Association.......	1898	1.75	.50	1.00	65	10	40
Norwalk.......	Elastic Goring Weavers.........	1885	3.50	1.50	1.75	55	5	......
Norwich	Loom Fixers Union	1889	1.88	1.70	1.80	60	6¼	49
"	Mule Spinners Union...........	1889	2.00	1.58	1.70	60	6¼	49
"	Weavers Union..................	1898	1.58	.37	1.00	60	6¼	49
"	Beamer Tenders Union.........	1898	1.75	1.50	1.60	60	6¼	49

TYPOGRAPHICAL UNION.

New Haven...	Typographical Union No. 47....	1860	4.16	2.50	3.00	59	9	52
Norwich	Typographical Union No. 100...	1867	3.50	2.50	3.00	59	9	52
Hartford......	Typographical Union No. 127...	1883	3.50	2.50	3.00	59	9	52
Bridgeport....	Typographical Union No. 252...	1889	3.00	2.00	2.50	59	9	52
Danbury......	Typographical Union No. 143...	1897	3.00	2.00	2.50	59	9	52
Meriden.......	Typographical Union No.	1892	3.00	2.40	2.50	60	10	52

WOODWORKERS.

Hartford......	Amalgamated Woodworkers...	1896	3.50	2.00	2.25	54	9	50

The preceding tables give the names of organizations, where located, highest, lowest and average of standard of wages, weekly hours of labor, hours employed on Saturday, and the average number of weeks employed per annum.

It is found that of the "outdoor" workers, the painters and stone masons lose the most time, their average being only 35 weeks in the year. Of the "indoor" workers, the tailors average but 26 weeks and the hatters 30 weeks in the year. This is explained by the fact that their work is governed by what is called "season work."

The highest, lowest and standard wage by trades is found to be as follows:

	Highest.	Lowest.	Standard.
Bakers	$3 50	$1 25	$2 25
Barbers	2 50	1 65	2 00
Beamer Tenders	1 75	1 50	1 60
Bookbinders	3 25	2 25	2 75
Brass Moulders	3 00	2 25	2 50
Brewers	3 33	2 00	2 50
Bricklayers	4 00	3 50	3 75
Buffers	3 00	2 00	2 50
Carpenters	3 00	1 50	2 50
Cigarmakers	3 75	1 50	2 25
Cotton Spinners	2 00	1 58	1 70
Cotton Weavers	1 75	50	1 10
Drivers	2 50	1 50	1 75
Electrical Workers	3 00	2 50	2 50
Elastic Goring Weavers	3 50	1 50	1 75
Hat Finishers	5 00	1 50	2 00
Horse Nail Workers	3 50	1 50	1 50
Horseshoers	3 50	2 00	2 50
House Painters	3 00	2 00	2 50
Iron Moulders	4 00	1 50	2 25
Locomotive Engineers	4 50	2 00	3 50
Loom Fixers	1 88	1 70	1 80
Machinists	4 00	2 00	2 75
Plumbers	3 50	2 00	2 75
Printers	4 16	2 00	2 50
Printing Pressmen	5 50	2 25	2 75
Railway Trainmen	3 00	1 50	2 00
Silk Weavers	1 75	50	1 00
Stationary Engineers	4 50	2 00	3 00
Stone Masons	3 87	3 00	3 00
Tailors	2 50	1 50	2 00
Woodworkers (machine)	3 50	2 00	2 25

TOTAL NUMBER ORGANIZED AND NUMBER UNEMPLOYED—INCREASE OF WAGES—DECREASE OF HOURS.

Trade or calling.	Number organized.				Number unemployed.			Benefits derived.	
	Number of organizations.	Men.	Women.	Total.	Men.	Women.	Total.	Increased wages.	Shorter hours.
Bakers	6	163	....	163	15	....	15	4	4
Barbers	4	87	....	87	1	....	1	1	2
Brewers	3	79	....	79	2	....	2	4	3
Buffers	4	795	....	795	45	....	45	3	1
Carpenters	9	1,224	....	1,224	146	....	146	6	7
Cigarmakers	11	754	3	757	44	....	44	10	10
Hatters	9	2,627	1,123	3,750	570	224	794	7	2
Horseshoers	2	30	....	30	....	....	....	1	2
Iron Moulders	10	552	....	552	24	....	24	8	1
Locomotive Engineers	3	378	....	378	20	....	20	3	3
Machinists	4	237	....	237	....	....	....	3	....
Miscellaneous	12	902	109	1,011	33	....	33	7	5
Musicians	5	345	4	349	....	....	....	5	....
Plumbers	5	163	....	163	48	....	48	3	3
Printers	6	305	13	318	43	1	44	6	4
Printing Pressmen	2	45	....	45	....	....	....	....	1
Railway Trainmen	4	276	....	276	....	....	....	4	3
Textiles	6	336	187	523	15	3	18	3	3
Total	105	9,298	1,439	10,737	1,004	228	1,232	78	54

This table summarizes the membership by sex, the number unemployed, the number of unions which have had wages increased, and the number of unions which have had the hours of labor decreased as a result of organization. The table represents the 105 unions which made reports. The first column gives the name of the organization and the second the number of unions of that craft. The number of male members is 9,298 and females 1,439. The total membership is 10,737. Of the males 1,004, or 10.9 per cent., and females 228, or 15.8 per cent., were out of employment at the time the report was made. The total number out of employment was 1,232, or 11.5 per cent. The number of unions which have had wages increased since, and as a result of, organization is 78, and the number which have had the hours of labor shortened is 54. A study of the returns shows that the increase in wages was secured by 12 strikes, 33 demands and 33 by action of the employers on petition of the employes. The decrease in hours of labor has been secured largely by the action of the National bodies of the several crafts forbidding their members to work beyond a specified time.

NOTES FROM THE UNIONS.

BAKE-SHOPS.

HARTFORD.—BAKERS AND CONFECTIONERS INTERNATIONAL UNION NO. 8.

The only suggestion we have to make is that there be a well conducted labor agitation. Anything else in our trade is of no benefit, because the "bosses" sign a contract and after a few weeks are over discharge the union men for some cause or other. Therefore, as above mentioned, agitation in favor of the union label is the only means to uphold the union and strengthen our craft. The union label certifies that the product bearing it is made in a clean, sanitary shop, under union rules.

BRIDGEPORT.—BAKERS AND CONFECTIONERS INTERNATIONAL UNION NO. 38.

What will improve our craft? I answer, a strict enforcement of the "Bake-shop law," passed by our last legislature, for clean and healthy shops.

In this city there are two bakers' unions, besides the one to which I belong. Both are independent, have no national head, and have no affiliation with organized labor. They are joined together to cut wages. They will not listen to labor talkers, or even go to a meeting called for their benefit.

BARBERS.

DANBURY.—JOURNEYMEN BARBERS INTERNATIONAL UNION OF AMERICA, LODGE NO 175.

Sunday closing would greatly benefit our craft. The hours of labor, if reduced from twelve to ten hours for a day's work, would also greatly improve our condition. There would be no need to reduce our pay of $2.00 per day, which is little enough.

MERIDEN.—JOURNEYMEN BARBERS INTERNATIONAL UNION OF AMERICA, LODGE NO. 88.

Organized barbers' unions should consist of all barbers who have served a three years' apprenticeship. Barber schools should be abolished.

NORWICH.—NATIONAL BARBERS ASSOCIATION NO. 26.

Our craft can best be helped by the barbers who are not members of a union becoming such.

NEW LONDON.—JOURNEYMEN BARBERS INTERNATIONAL UNION NO. 136.

We desire a barbers' license law, as in some other States, requiring persons having practiced the trade in this or in another State for at least three years, and is possessed of the requisite skill in said trade to properly perform all the duties thereof; to register within ninety days from date of passage, punishing any one without a certificate, by a fine or imprisonment, or both. Study the trade as an apprentice under a qualified and practical barber, whether in a shop or a student in barber schools; all to be examined by a board of examiners. Under such laws and regulations, you would have skilled workmen, which would be a benefit and protection to the patrons, as well as those who have to compete with unskilled and cheap labor.

BRASS MOULDERS.

MERIDEN.

We should like steady employment, except during the vacation period in January and July. Eight hours' pay for eight hours' work is the general desire of the Brass Moulders' Union.

BREWERS.

MERIDEN.

We want shorter hours per day and more thorough organization.

HARTFORD.

If people would purchase only the stock that bears the union label it would help our organization. The label is a guarantee that the product has been made by union men.

BRICKLAYERS AND PLASTERERS.

HARTFORD.—UNION NO. 1 OF CONNECTICUT.

Organization has been of great benefit to us, as before we formed the union we were working ten hours a day for whatever wages we could get. Now we work but nine hours and receive not less than $3.50 for a day's work. Some receive $4.00, but the majority receive $3.75.

BUFFERS AND POLISHERS.

BRIDGEPORT.

To have every buffer and polisher a member of our union will help us more than anything else.

CARPENTERS AND JOINERS.

HARTFORD.—UNITED BROTHERHOOD OF CARPENTERS AND JOINERS NO. 43.

Organization has been a benefit to the carpenters and joiners in this city, as it has reduced the hours of labor per week. Union men are also receiving fifty cents a day more than non-union men. The apprenticeship system would also be of benefit to us. As an organized body we have had no strike for any cause.

NEW BRITAIN.—NO. 27.

Organization here has not been of as much benefit as it ought to be. The reason, no doubt is, is because we are, as a trade, not fully organized. To be fully benefited our craft should have in its union membership all the carpenters in the town, or nearly all. If we had three-quarters of them we would be in a position to demand better wages and get them.

One of the worst features of our trade is the lack of thoroughly efficient workmen. To correct and avoid this condition it would be helpful if the apprenticeship system was established by enactment of the legislature of a law compelling a person to learn the trade before offering himself as a tradesman. The law should compel every workman to show, when asked, a certificate of his ability, and the certificate should bear the seal of the county.

BRIDGEPORT.—NO. 115.

If all the journeymen carpenters were in our organization, our wages would be $3.00 per day of nine hours.

The contractors are in favor of organization. It is the men's fault that cheap labor reigns supreme here. Our city directory shows 560 men classed as carpenters.

NORWALK.—NO. 746.

It would greatly benefit our craft if the laws regarding liens on buildings could be amended so that a journeyman could get his wages where an irresponsible contractor fails to pay his men, for the reason that he has taken a contract for a less price than a responsible one could have taken it and pay for his labor and material.

This would make people more careful about who they let contracts to. It would benefit responsible contractors as well as the journeymen, if the journeymen could contract his wages from the owner of the building.

Our experience here is that if one can possibly collect his wages from one of this class of contractors, it usually costs more than the wages amount to.

The journeymen carpenters are alone to blame that they do not get their share of the good things of this world, by not coming into the union and being thoroughly organized for their own benefit. Our craft certainly furnishes more tools, more brains and runs more risk of loss of life than any other branch of the building trade, or any other trade, and we receive about the least wages for our labor.

DERBY.—NO. 127.

Organization is the keynote to our success in trying to better our condition. This union is only in its infancy. We are trying to get a complete organization so that when we attempt to get higher wages and shorter hours we shall be reasonably sure of success. We aim not only to get our hours of labor reduced, but to maintain the present rate of wages.

I believe that reducing the hours of labor is a matter of prime importance, because it gives employment to a greater number of men, hence more money in circulation and more business. Where there is a demand for labor, wages will adjust themselves.

MERIDEN.—NO. 2.

At the present time our union is in poor condition owing to two reasons. Trade is at a standstill here and many of our members have sought work elsewhere. Our laws provide that if a member takes jobs, or contracts for three months, he shall lose his standing in the union. Most of our members have had to do this—become contractors—in order to live. Consequently we have lost in membership so many that we hold no regular meetings. The Central Labor Union, however, attends to matters for us and gives attention to all grievances and by so doing holds for us the ground we gained by organization.

I know of no union man wholly out of employment, as the public have come to understand that the most devoted union man is the most likely to be the best mechanic and do his work well.

Jealousy among workingmen is the worst thing we have to contend with, for if one is active in all the branches of organized labor, he is said to be "after something" for himself. There is nothing that will help us so much as education will along these lines, and I sincerely believe that there is no better educator in this country, save the church, than the labor union. The man who becomes a member of one of these unions with the sole view in his mind of helping to improve the condition of his fellowman, will find his own improving and his own happiness increasing.

CIGARMAKERS.

NEW HAVEN.—CIGARMAKERS INTERNATIONAL UNION OF AMERICA NO. 39.

Organization has increased wages and shortened the hours of labor.

A strike was made for the increase of wages. It is believed that nearly all members of the craft in this city are members of the union. The members will be benefited by the enforcement of the "Trade Label Law" and the enactment of a strict sanitary law.

HARTFORD.—NO. 42.

By organization wages have been increased and hours of labor decreased, both being secured by a strike after a request had been made and refused. Before the formation of the union wages were from 25 per cent. to 30 per cent. less than now. As far as known all members of the craft in this section are organized. As to what would improve the condition of the craft, I am of the opinion that the abolition of the tenement house cigar factory would be of vast benefit to our craft, and also to the smoking public, who are liable to contract disease from the product of such factories. Hon. Theodore Roosevelt, Assistant Secretary of War, when he was a member of the New York State Assembly, spoke as follows on the bill to prohibit the making of cigars in tenement houses: "I have visited these pestholes personally, and I can assure you if smokers could only see how these cigars are made we would not need any legislation against this system at all." The New York *Sun* had this to say under the caption of "The Cigars of Death:" "The tenement house inspectors, now making their rounds, have found nothing in any quarter of New York more dangerous to public health, family virtue and common decency than the huge tenement house cigar factories which have frequently, during the past few years, been forced upon the notice of the Board of Health, but which, for some reason—through some means—are still allowed to exist"

We have persistently sought to get legislative action against this system wherever it existed, but without much success. However, we have been more successful in fighting this system since the adoption of our blue label, more especially in the past ten years, when our label has become better known. This label, when placed upon a box of cigars, is a guarantee that the cigars contained therein have been made under clean and healthy conditions.

SOUTH NORWALK.

Wages were increased and hours decreased by the manufacturers when request for the same was made to them after we organized a union in this city. There are about forty unorganized men at work here. They receive from $1.00 to $3.00 per week less than the others. Continuous agitation in favor of the use of goods bearing the "Union Label," which is a guarantee of their being made in a clean shop, will greatly assist the craft. Sale of prison-made cigars should be prohibited.

LONG HILL.—NO. 139.

Organization has been of decided benefit to us, as a craft, as our wages have been increased and the hours shortened as a result of such action. Both were granted by the employers when asked for. All cigarmakers in town are members of the union. Prison labor should be abolished and not be allowed to compete in the market with fair and honest labor.

The craft would be strengthened and greatly helped if all would purchase only goods bearing the "Blue Label," which is evidence that they have been made in a clean and sanitary shop.

DANBURY.—NO. 180.

Since the cigarmakers' union was formed here our wages have been increased, and we do not have to put in so many hours per day. We have had no strike or difficulty with our employers. There are but two cigarmakers in the place who do not belong to the union. There should be laws preventing the employment of child and prison labor. The Bureau of Labor Statistics should be continued and have the same support as does the Board of Agriculture and other State departments.

SUFFIELD.—NO. 156.

Wages were raised and hours decreased after a strike. We consider organization a great benefit. All cigarmakers here are members of the union.

ANSONIA.—NO. 103.

In 1886 a demand was made for an increase of wages, which was granted. We have had no occasion to strike. Our working time has also been decreased. All members of the craft here are members of the union.

Thorough organization of workingmen in every branch of trade and calling will naturally improve the condition of our craft, inasmuch as organized labor recognizes only union-made goods.

We believe unions are equally good for manufacturers and employes. Manufacturers in a locality, who run strictly union shops, have no advantage over one another in the matter of wages, as they are governed alike by the scale of prices they pay, as far as wages are concerned. They cannot cut prices to any great extent on finished products, as the cost of manufacture, etc., is nearly the same, thus proving that it is equally good for both employer and employe.

Now, on the other hand, how is it with non-union manufacturers? They are not governed by any union scale of prices. They pay their employes what they will take, which generally is a great deal less than union wages. In this way such a manufacturer will, because of less cost of manufacture, to secure trade, sell his goods for less the difference of wages than his union competitor; so where is the advantage or benefit he has derived? His goods cost him less, but he also sells them for less. We fail to see where it is any benefit to run a non-union shop. The only thing they can say is that they can hire employes at any wages they see fit to pay them, and perhaps they consider it to their advantage to run factories under conditions which would not be tolerated by union people, as the same has cost the unions many thousands of dollars in various ways to abolish.

BRIDGEPORT.—NO. 282.

We have had our wages increased and secured a shorter workingday by organization. We have had two strikes, the first being for an increase of wages, and was successful. The second was for the enforcement of union regulations, and was only partially successful. Our weekly wages average $8.08 per week on an actual working time of 32 hours per week.

NEW LONDON.—NO. 189.

While our hours have been decreased as a result of organization, wages have not improved. Unorganized men are working as low as $8.00 per week. What we lack is a thorough organization. More are out of the union than in. The city is full of scab goods. If union men would stop buying them and purchase only those goods bearing the union label it would be of great benefit to the cigarmakers' union, which stands for clean goods made in clean places.

WATERBURY.—NO. 395.

Previous to organization the members of the craft residing in Waterbury were members of Union No. 103, at Ansonia. All work here is regulated by the union scale. We work on the piece system. There are but four cigarmakers here who are not union men. They receive from $2.00 to $5.00 per week less than union men do. We consider organization as a benefit to us.

NORWICH.—NO. 407.

Our wages have been increased and daily working hours decreased as a result of organization. Both were granted us by the manufacturers without trouble. There are about twelve men who are not yet in the union here. A better patronage of the "Blue Label" goods will help us more than anything else.

ELECTRICAL WORKERS.

HARTFORD.—BROTHERHOOD OF ELECTRICAL WORKERS OF AMERICA, LOCAL NO. 37.

For the improvement of the condition of our craft I would suggest the establishment of a State law governing an apprentice system. I would also favor the licensing of all men professing to be first-class electrical workers, after putting each and every one through an examination, this examination not to be on purely technical subjects, but on matters pertaining to trade, and issue a license accordingly. Some time ago the local to which I belong, brought before the ordinance committee of this city a bill in which the above conditions were stated, together with numerous remarks from prominent iusurance men of this city, and a meeting was called of the above-mentioned committee at which meeting our bill was ordered tabled and we were told that we would be notified when it came up. After waiting about two months without hearing from the committee we started a committee out to send a tracer after the bill, with the result that up to the present time we have not been able to find out what happened to it. In bringing this matter before my organization I was instructed to request you, as far as it were possible for you to do, to help us get this bill passed. If at any time you should desire other information about this or any other matter, I assure you that by writing me I will do all in my power to aid you.

LOCOMOTIVE ENGINEERS.

NEW HAVEN.

As the rate of wages varies according to the service performed, the scale paid the New Haven division is here given as an illustration of the method of apportionment.

"The engineers on the New Haven system of the N. Y., N. H. & H. R. R. work under a written contract, which we denote a schedule, signed by the company on their part and a committee of engineers on our part, which is termed the mileage system. It originated with our organization, and we consider it the fairest and most equitable system that has yet been introduced, equally as just for the company as for the engineers, viz.: 100 miles or less constitutes a day's work on passenger or freight trains, 3½ cents per mile for passenger and 4 cents per mile for freight trains; work trains $100 per month of 26 working days. Hours are not considered in passenger trains as they run on schedule time. On most of the divisions freights are paid overtime if out over 12 hours, time to begin at 10 hours at the rate of 35 cents per hour; also work trains are paid overtime under the same ruling as regards hours for freights. A day's pay is $3.50 for passenger and $4.00 for freight. Firemen promoted to engineers are paid on switch engines $2.50 first year, $3.00 second year and $3.50 third year, 8 hours to constitute a day's work; all over time pro rata. If assigned to road work, to be paid the rate as per schedule in the class in which they are employed. This rate applies to the New York, Hartford, Shore Line, Air Line, Shepang, and New Haven divisions; the Berkshire, Danbury & Norwalk and Naugatuck divisions work under what is called the trip system, which also includes overtime after being out a given number of hours. The rate runs from $3 00 to $7.00 per day. The $7.00 rate is a long day's work for an engineer and is divided between two men running alternate days. All things being considered, the Brotherhood of Locomotive Engineers favor the mileage system and the privileges that it confers on them in preference to any other system of pay. In the aggregate they are the gainers both in hours of labor and a higher rate of pay."

STATIONARY ENGINEERS.

MERIDEN.—NATIONAL ASSOCIATION OF STATIONARY ENGINEERS NO. 1, OF CONNECTICUT.

The National Association of Stationary Engineers is in no sense a labor organization in the usual acceptance of the term, therefore this fact precludes the possibility of definitely answering all of the questions required in the schedule.

Education is the first consideration—in fact, the foundation stone of our order and the principle for which we are united. We realize that the interests of the manufacturer (employer) and the engineer are identical. The more economically and efficiently that an engineer can operate a steam plant the more useful he is both to himself and his employer, and we have found that sooner or later true merit meets with just recognition and reward.

Our weekly meetings are devoted largely to the consideration of practical questions relating to the generation and transmission of power and kindred subjects.

There is one desideratum, namely, an honest engineer's license law. That such laws, requiring that every operating or superintending engineer in the State of Connecticut shall demonstrate his ability to safely control the enormous natural forces with which he has to deal, also to prove himself able to successfully meet any emergency arising in the plant under his charge, would be greatly beneficial to employer and engineer alike there cannot be the slightest doubt, as the results of such laws, enacted by Massachusetts, New York City and other communities throughout the United States bear witness. For years the subordinate associations of this State have been striving for such laws and sooner or later these laws must come.

Regarding wages, would state that we have no "scale," rather believing that merit will be met with just and sufficient compensation. Some of the members of this subordinate association are qualified to take full charge of any steam plant in the State, and some have never had charge of anything larger than a twenty horse-power plant. The question of wages is not given the first consideration by our organization. In many instances wages have been voluntarily increased, or at least increased for the mere asking, after certain members have been with us for a year or so, due to the greater knowledge of the profession which they have attained through the educational feature which is given the first consideration in our order.

Engineers, as a rule, have a great deal of work to attend to that cannot be done in running hours, also more or less time to devote to their plants on Sundays, such as cleaning boilers, making extensive repairs or adjustments to engines and steam appliances, which is part and parcel of the duties of an engineer and for which, usually, there is no extra compensation. On the other hand whenever a holiday of any kind turns up the time of the engineer is his to use as his judgment dictates, provided, first of all, that his plant does not need his attention in any of its details.

HATMAKERS.

DANBURY.—HATMAKERS OF DANBURY.

Our craft is much different from any other, as we have what we call Fall and Spring trade, which lately has lasted about ten weeks each. The remainder of the year we have parts of the day perhaps, which would be from 60 cents to $1.20 for the time worked. Take for instance the shop which I am employed in. There has been no work in it since the 15th of April, 1898, and no prospects of any until after the 15th of July, when the Fall trade usually starts. Before the depression $3 was considered the day's wages for the average man (though there were men who could make $4), and when it went under that there was a grievance, which was investigated, and if it was found the manufacturer was at fault he would be compelled to either pay more per dozen or change his mixtures so that men could do enough to bring their wages up to that standard, the men remaining at work pending the settlement. There are some branches of the trade at the present time, where men have full work, at which $5.00 or $6.00 per day can be made, but they are very few. The majority make from $2.00 to $2.50 in good times. You can see from the amount of work they have in a year that it is impossible to live on that. The only way I can see that our craft can be benefited is for the manufacturers to stop cutting each other in the market, or the people of the country to patronize hats that bear the union label of the United Hatters of North America, as that insures the purchaser that the men making them receive the best wages, and that they receive more than in the shops of firms who pay what they please to their help, and if they say anything against it are discharged. Others take their places, and for what the manufacturers choose to pay them. If such firms as these did not receive the patronage of the people they would be compelled to make their factories fair, pay fair wages, and could not go into the market with the advantage they now have over manufacturers who are disposed to deal fairly with their employes. There is much that could be said on what would be a benefit to the hatting trade, but I must content myself with what I have said.

DANBURY.—HAT FINISHERS ASSOCIATION.

Encourage organized labor by purchasing only such goods as bear the union label when they are to be had.

NORWALK.—HATMAKERS ASSOCIATION.

The Hatmakers Association allows members to work only by the piece, except the foreman and one assistant. Ten hours constitute a day's labor, to be done between the hours of 7 A. M. and 6 P. M. The association says all work must cease at 12 o'clock, noon, on Saturday.

The United Hatters of North America is composed of about 5,000 members, and is supported by the different local hatters' associations. It has had for a number of years a label, to be placed in all union-made hats, and we believe it has been a great success. The association advocates the purchase of all union-made goods. We favor an eight-hour law.

NORWALK.—HAT FINISHERS.

An increased demand on the part of the consumers for goods bearing our union label. Our wages and conditions are not such as skilled mechanics should enjoy. But we realize that there are many whose necessities compel them to exchange their labor for even less than we receive. We have not even a fighting chance to improve our wages. We might succeed in forcing manufacturers to raise our wages, thereby making it harder for them to meet the competition of the employers of cheap and unorganized labor. But we feel that this policy would eventually work their ruin and ours too.

HORSESHOERS.

NEW HAVEN.—JOURNEYMEN HORSESHOERS UNION NO. 26.

Horseshoeing is hard work, and I would like to see ten hours form a day's work for five days and five hours on Saturdays.

ANSONIA.—JOURNEYMEN HORSESHOERS UNION NO. 87.

In answer to your last question I will state, for myself, that education will improve the condition of any craft, for the more we read and study the better we can find a way to improve the condition of our craft and ourselves. It also opens a way for expressing our opinions on any subject that may come before us for discussion. The labor question is something that needs lots of study, and we must not jump at conclusions too soon, for we are all liable to be mistaken sometimes. We must go at this labor question in a cool manner so that we may all understand it when it is brought before us for discussion. Educate your men on this question and they will soon find a way to improve their condition.

Now, in regard to wages by the day, there are two branches of workmen in the horseshoeing trade who are known as the firemen and the floormen. The former receive more pay than the latter, so you will see by my figures that a fireman receives $3 a day and a floorman $2 a day. In regard to working hours we always worked ten hours on Saturday until our union was organized, and when we asked for nine hours on Saturday we got it right away.

In regard to benefits of organized labor there are a good many. In the first place it brings men together for the purpose of bettering their condition in life, not only socially, but financially. It creates a good feeling, and that is always necessary to make a success of anything you undertake to do. We had a case right here in our own union. Two men who had not spoken a word to each other for two years became members of the union, and to-day they are working hand in hand for the benefit of the union.

IRON MOULDERS.

ANSONIA.—IRON MOULDERS UNION OF NORTH AMERICA NO. 89.

It has long been a mooted question as to how to secure justice to the day wage-worker. In many of the trades where good organization prevails a reasonable amount of justice has been secured, but the trades of lesser organization the men are at the mercy of the employers. Often even a hearing is denied them. Many times men make mistakes by not giving attention to surrounding or distant economic conditions, but in the cases I now have in mind, even if they were thus fortified, it would avail them little personally.

In disputes between employer and employe I believe there should be a board possessing judicial power and making attendance compulsory on part of employer and employe. This board, having power to determine, should also have power to enforce their decisions. This may not be a solution of the labor problem, but it would at least cause the employer to recognize the reasonable claims of his employes, and not needlessly destroy the peaceful serenity of our different localities.

BRIDGEPORT.—NO. 110.

That which will be of the most benefit to our craft is a thorough organization. This accomplished, we shall secure a workingday of eight hours, and thereby give an opportunity for some of the idle ones — not from choice — to secure work. Another help would be the restriction of immigration.

The curse of our business is the piece system, which prevails in most shops. Our trade is filling up with Hungarians and Poles who are willing to work cheaper than the English-speaking people can. They live very cheap; in fact, in a manner that is a disgrace to civilization. It is humiliating, to say the least, to American manhood and womanhood to be obliged to compete with them, let alone having to endure their presence which is often revolting in the extreme, and I must add that it is such people that get the preference with some of our manufacturers.

The majority of them do not intend to remain here. They accumulate until they have sufficient to buy land where they came from and then they return. Others then come and take their places. If any of them die the town generally has to bury them.

You may think this is not so, but I assure you that it is. Shame to us that our American-born young men are walking the streets for lack of employment on account of these people being given the preference. Many of them have enlisted and are now fighting for our country and its flag. These people will not do that; they did not come here for that purpose. I might say much more but will refrain from doing so as I think I have given the Labor Commissioner some idea of our grievance.

HARTFORD.—NO. 72.

More thorough organization is the most important of the thousand and one suggestions that may be offered for the betterment of our condition.

ROCKY HILL.—NO. 302.

If our organization was more thoroughly organized it would be more beneficial to the members of our craft. We would have less strikes, and the money spent in strikes if spent in perfecting organization, would secure better wages and shorter hours. Our firm tells us that they cannot compete with firms making the same class of goods because they have to pay higher wages to union men.

Every iron moulder should be a union man. There should be a paid organizer to visit about for the purpose of adding to the unions. Our organization has been visited but once since its formation.

MACHINISTS.

BRIDGEPORT.—INTERNATIONAL ASSOCIATION OF MACHINISTS.

To my mind organization outclasses all reforms offered for the betterment of the laboring classes, save some form of socialism. Free trade, with the single tax, high tariff or low tariff have proved fruitless to stem the tide of falling wages. The single tax is being tried in New Zealand, I believe, and from reports the results obtained are not to be compared with what could be obtained by organized labor thoroughly organized. The reasons Bridgeport is so poorly organized are various. Some cannot bear the thought of the financial investment required, while othere are fearful that if their employers knew of their joining the union their jobs would be jeopardized, while the bulk, I must say, are not awake to the real necessity of the times. Few of the laboring class know anything of political economy, in fact hardly know the application of the same. We of Bridgeport believe in shortening the number of hours for a day's work, thereby employing the surplus and opening chances for better pay made by the increased demand for labor.

NEW BRITAIN.—INTERNATIONAL ASSOCIATION OF MACHINISTS.

An eight-hour day with eight hours' pay would be a great benefit to our trade. We also desire to see the apprenticeship system introduced, which would be a surety that all machinists were capable, trained men. The system would also be of inestimable benefit to the public as well as the trade.

BRIDGEPORT.—MACHINISTS AND TOOLMAKERS ASSOCIATION.

Thorough organization of the machinists and toolmakers under one head, working for the benefit of each other, with no heavy values to pay, and the dues heavy enough to have a substantial weekly benefit in case of sickness or disability. A competent committee to arbitrate all grievances so as to avoid a strike if possible. A more friendly feeling to a new hand coming into a shop—in fact a living down of the petty jealousies that exist, I am sorry to say, to a greater extent than one not in the trade is aware of.

I would like to say just a few words on the subject of unionism in the machinists and toolmakers' trades. We have been in existence now nearly seven years, first as a local union for two years, then we were affiliated with the International Machinists' Union three years, and for the last two years we have been just a local benefit association, doing our best to organize the men, and, I tell you, it is an uphill, thankless job in this city. But there are a few of us that think we know what a thorough organization would mean for us all, and we dislike to give it up.

MUSICAL PROTECTIVE UNION.

BRIDGEPORT.—AMERICAN FEDERATION OF MUSICIANS NO. 63.

Musicians, though not strictly a trade union, should certainly organize to assist the other class of wage-workers. We have splendid success, because we do not have corporations and monopolies to fight, but deal more with individuals. In this city, for instance, we have given the unions the biggest boom they have had for years, and will continue to do so. We are the only body of musicians in this State with a national head. The other locals would improve greatly should they join the American Federation of Musicians, 20,000 strong.

DANBURY.

I think it would be well, if practical, to establish a bill of prices in all musical unions in the State, the same price to be paid in each city for all engagements of the same character.

The musicians of this city are obliged to compete with union musicians of other cities, and have to play at lower prices than we play the same business at home or lose the business. I refer, of course, to business outside of our own city.

SOUTH NORWALK.

Our union, although a young organization, is at present in a thriving condition, and I can think of no suggestion whereby the members could be benefited. We are striving to get the applications of the few non-union musicians in town, and hope soon to have every player of ability in the organization.

PLUMBERS.

HARTFORD.—UNITED ASSOCIATION OF JOURNEYMEN PLUMBERS.

It would be a great help to plumbers if the city ordinances in regard to registering plumbers were put into effect by the Board of Health. As it now stands apprentices do a great deal of the work that journeymen ought to be doing, thereby throwing skilled men out of work. This is the sentiment of every journeyman plumber, union or non-union, in Hartford.

MERIDEN.—PLUMBERS, GAS AND STEAM FITTERS UNION.

We need the passage of a law by the State that would require a strict inspection of all plumbing by inspectors who are masters of this trade in all its branches.

NORWICH.—PLUMBERS, GAS AND STEAM FITTERS UNION.

Trade is very dull in this vicinity. Owing to this fact and that we have been organized but a short time we have made no effort to have wages increased. The master plumbers cut prices in competition with each other, and this has a tendency to keep wages down. There are a great many journeymen here who have not yet united with the union. Some say they can get along without union membership. We still hope to induce them to unite with us.

NEW BRITAIN.—UNITED ASSOCIATION OF JOURNEYMEN PLUMBERS.

We want a State law that will compel plumbers to pass an examination and take out a license. This will improve our craft and be a still greater benefit to the public health.

NEW HAVEN.—PLUMBERS, GAS AND STEAM FITTERS UNION.

We need more thorough organization of all journeymen plumbers. As it is now, men have to take what wages are offered.

PRINTING PRESSMEN.

HARTFORD.—NO. 75.

A shorter workday without reduction of wages. Other trades have it, and I think we should also, as I believe as much work would be done under ordinary circumstances in a nine-hour day as is done in ten hours. I do not think the employers would lose anything in the long run, and the shorter workday would help them as well as the pressmen, as they would be able to make up for it in better prices for work without any perceptible difference in the amount of work finished, as the whole thing amounts to a raise in wages and would spur the pressmen on, and they would work the harder, and the result would be satisfactory to the employers as well as the employes.

SHOEMAKERS.

DANBURY.—SHOEMAKERS PROTECTIVE UNION.

The largest number of members of our organization are self-employing. But notwithstanding that, when the trade was not organized, there was a strong tendency to lower the price charged for the work done by the several shoemakers, and therefore partially reducing the profit—that is, their wages. Since we organized we have a standard price for the different kinds of work we do, based on a fair day's wages.

The difference between the cost of material employed and expense (rent, light, heat. etc.), and the price charged for work is our wages, being the share due for the work we perform.

STONE MASONS.

HARTFORD.—UNION NO. 7, OF CONNECTICUT.

About seven years ago the stone masons were receiving forty cents per hour. Our work is very hard, and on account of the weather we lose a large amount of time. We struck for forty-five cents per hour. The "bosses" offered forty-three cents. We held out for one year, and did not consider the strike a success. Our organization has been of benefit to us, but we are troubled by outsiders coming in to work for less than union rates. I mean unorganized labor ; and if they will work for less than the standard rate there is always some contractor ready to hire cheap labor. Some are working as low as twenty-five cents per hour. As high as forty-three is paid by some of the "bosses," but the standard rate is forty cents. Those receiving the lower rate are inferior workmen.

I am opposed to strikes except when there is no other way. Every means possible should be tried before a strike is ordered.

TEXTILE WORKERS.

NORWICH.—NATIONAL LOOM FIXERS.

We favor a national eight-hour day law.

NORWICH.—NATIONAL MULE SPINNERS ASSOCIATION.

We had quite a lot of trouble lately. We had a two-weeks' strike against a reduction of ten per cent. The strike brought it to an average of eight, and was the cause of organizing the weavers and part of the carding room, and I am under the impression that they mean to keep it up, for they have seen how it would have benefited them if they had been organized about one year ago. They would have been able to resist the reduction much better.

Looking at the depression of the cotton trade at the present time, in my humble opinion it would be a good thing to lessen the hours of labor in factories. It would help our trade and benefit the men, women and children employed, as well as have a tendency to prolong our lives. I would like to know why they want us to work ten hours a day in factories, in a congested atmosphere, when the masons, carpenters and others, out doors, only work nine hours. There is nothing to remedy this but organization and the ballot.

NORWICH.—WEAVERS.

Having been organized only a short time, organization has not yet shown the benefit of such action. The employers have taken advantage of our not being organized to cut and cut our wages, not a general plan, but in changing weaving from time to time to different patterns. Shorter hours would help us. Our reason for desiring this is that the manufacturers tell us "the market is overstocked." Shorter hours will lessen the production and create a larger demand for woven goods and give more regular employment. Better wages can also be paid.

BRIDGEPORT.—SILK WORKERS ASSOCIATION.

Pass a law that will punish employers who discharge their employes who join labor organizations.

Also a law that shall make nine hours a legal day's work, except Saturday, when it shall be eight.

This will reduce production and give a chance for the surplus labor to be used, and then with a better demand we shall receive better wages. This will not only benefit the employes, but the general public as well.

The only way for the industrial classes of this country to

better their condition is to organize for the purpose of protection and education. They should seek such legislation as will work for their betterment, which, in many cases, is most desirable.

NORWALK.—ELASTIC GORING WEAVERS AMALGAMATED ASSOCIATION.

Our branch has had no local strike. We have had, however, three strikes in the trade against a reduction of wages and were successful each time.

Our trade has been in a very depressed condition for the last five years on account of the change of style of shoes. I do not think we have averaged more than two days a week during that time.

TYPOGRAPHICAL UNION.

NEW HAVEN.—NO. 47.

The enrollment of all non-union men in this city of our trade would be of great benefit to us and also to the non-unionists.

I think a shorter workday would be of great benefit to the workingmen of this country. It would certainly, if it became adopted by workingmen generally throughout the country, give employment to some of that "vast army of unemployed" we hear so much about.

NORWICH.—NO. 100.

A shorter workingday would furnish employment for the surplus printers of this country. The use of the union label would benefit us.

HARTFORD.—NO. 127.

To have all printed matter bear our label. If this is done the public will know that whenever work is done and bears this label the help employed on said work are receiving fair and living wages. We will never be satisfied until the above is accomplished.

Being reorganized since December 3, 1883, makes us in existence, next December, fifteen years. During this time we have had one strike, and we tried all possible means to avoid that. We do not believe in strikes. Our members in said strike were discharged one by one and girls put in their places, receiving from $6.00 to $9.00 per week.

Naturally most people will think since the introduction of machinery that we are losing ground. No. We are much stronger at the present time than six years ago, or thereabouts, when the Mergenthaler was introduced in our trade.

The only thing that will improve our condition is the label.

BRIDGEPORT.—NO. 252.

Members holding situations in newspaper offices have steady work all the year round, while those in job printing offices are generally on short time during the late summer and early fall. Eight hours constitute a day's labor on morning newspapers and nine and nine and one-half on evening. Our membership is continually fluctuating, through arrivals and withdrawals, but generally we have about half a dozen members not holding steady situations. Machinery, during the last two or three years, has considerably lessened our membership. A thorough organization of the printing trades, all branches, in this city, and working in harmony with proprietors, would improve conditions.

DANBURY.—NO. 143.

There is nothing that I can suggest under this head except that thorough organization, under present conditions, is the only thing that will improve the condition of the craft. Get all other trade unions to call for the typographical union label on their printing, and patronize only goods bearing the labels of fraternal organizations. If possible seek to better the wage-earners' condition by political ends, and gain points by legislation in the same manner that the firemen did when they got the State Firemen's Association incorporated.

In other words, get the workmen as well protected as are the gigantic corporations, holding valuable charters granted by the State.

MERIDEN.

At the present time all the printers in this city are employed, and are in complete harmony with the employers.

FROM A MERIDEN GLASS CUTTER.

That organization among the workingmen has been the means of elevating their condition is a fact which cannot be disputed.

It was through the influence of organized labor that the various States established the Bureaus of Labor Statistics to investigate and report the actual condition of the working classes with a view to improving the same. For that reason there can be found in our State to-day, as well as in others, men who have no sympathy for, or interest in, the elevation of the masses of the people (men whom the workingmen themselves elect to the legislatures to make laws for them), who would, if they had their way, abolish the offices of the Commissioner of Labor Statistics and Inspector of Factories entirely, knowing that the investigation and exposure of the unsanitary conditions of factories and mills, sweat-shops, dangerous and unguarded machinery, elevators, etc., would create an agitation and comment which would result in some action being taken to remedy the same.

It was through the influence and at the request of organized labor that laws were passed by the several States in the interest of education by restricting the employment of children of tender age in the factories and mills. It is a fact worthy of consideration that in States where there are no labor organizations to speak of (particularly in the South) neither are there any such laws on their statute books restricting child labor as in States where labor is well organized. This has been referred to by several of the leading newspapers recently in commenting on the great cotton mills strike throughout New England against a reduction of wages, and which led to an attempt by the owners of the mills in Massachusetts to have the laws restricting child labor in that State repealed by the last legislature in order that they might be better able to compete with the South. This could be properly classed as a movement in the interest of illiteracy.

I will quote from a paper read at the ninth annual convention of the International Association of Factory Inspectors, held at Providence, R. I., September 3, 1895, by Deputy Inspector Jordan, of New York, and who also presented a table originally prepared by Assistant Factory Inspector John Franey, of New York, entitled, "Table showing percentage of illiteracy, population, child labor, etc., in the United States." Mr. Jordan stated, among other things: "It is discouraging to find the illiteracy of North Carolina in 1890 as high as 37.7 per cent., while in 1850 the illiteracy of free negroes was only 21.32 per cent. and the whites only 13.30 per cent. It is surely no mere coincidence, but more likely cause and effect, that a State which has (proportionately) more than ten times the child labor of New York should have trebled its illiteracy during the last forty-five years, while the 'little red school-house,' in Fourth of July oratory at least, has been marching on in triumph everywhere else except, of course, in South Carolina. This State had 10.25 per cent. child labor and 45 per cent. illiteracy in 1890, but less than 10 per cent. free negroes illiterate and less than 6 per cent. among the whites before the war. Alabama also stands out with 40 per cent. illiteracy in 1890 and 4.50 per cent. child labor, but less than 11 per cent. of negroes and 8 per cent. of whites in 1850. Even Rhode Island, with over 8 per cent. child labor, had over 9 per cent. illiteracy in 1890, but only 7.27 per cent. for negroes and 2.32 per cent. of whites in 1850. This looks like the worst kind of reaction—certainly not like progress. * * * Is it not humiliating that California and Vermont should be worse than Belgium, Holland and Russia, àllowing children to work at 10 years, and that Maine and Rhode Island should not rise higher than the low limit of 12 years of those continental countries? That New Jersey and Louisiana should not rise to the level of France and Germany, that of 13 years? * * *"

The above is certainly a gloomy picture of the condition of the working classes in those and other States from an educational standpoint, and should receive earnest attention and action to remedy the same, not only from organized labor, but from our legislators and others who have any regard for the future welfare and greatness of our Nation.

It is written, "A Nation's greatness depends, not on acres, but upon the education of its people." In order to remedy the above and make other improvements in the condition of the working class of a permanent nature, and put them into effect, organized labor must discard its old policy and motto of "No politics," and adopt the reverse, "All politics," as it is only through legislation that the above and other permanent improvements can be accomplished. Workingmen themselves must be the legislators and the desired laws passed by their votes instead of begging of and trusting to others to do it for them. As evidence that organized labor has already taken this view, I will state that in 1897 seventeen unions affiliated with the State Branch American Federation of Labor, voted in favor of calling a convention for political action while only four voted against it.

PART III.

CONDITION OF MANUFACTURES.

1. Division by Industries and Establishments.

2. Persons Employed.

3. Wages.

4. Business Done.

5. Division by Localities.

CONDITION OF MANUFACTURES.

PART III. of this report is devoted to the condition of the manufacturing industries of the State, the investigation having been made along the same lines as last year, with the view that an intelligent comparison can be made with previous years, the same industries being considered.

It will be noticed that the number of establishments represented in the tabulation which follows is considerably less than the number which appeared in the chapter of the report for 1897 devoted to the same subject. This is explained in part by the fact that the means at the command of the Bureau were insufficient for the employment of the necessary assistance required to make a canvass of the entire State, and, furthermore, in the chapter of the report relating to the Textile Industries of Connecticut will be found a statistical abstract of the manufactures of cotton, hosiery, knit, silk and woolen goods, covering in a measure the same matters as are shown in Part III.

There are many reasons why meagre returns are given by some manufacturers and especially so when the period of unusual financial stringency and depression, which has prevailed in the State for some years past, is taken into consideration.

There is considerable pride among manufacturers regarding their business, and naturally there is some reluctance in making a return when the conditions of any year have been to their disadvantage. Some of those having capital invested in manufactories or mills feel that they could not make a good showing, and, perhaps, thoroughly disheartened, do not wish to make a report. It is pleasing to note, however, that as the aims and objects of the department become better understood there is less objection to answer the questions propounded. It should be stated here that as much consideration is given in the collection of the returns from an establishment employing five or six individuals as that from one with as many hundred employes. Those taken from small concerns are just as valuable for purposes of statistics as those gotten from the larger ones.

An improvement in industrial conditions is made manifest by the result of the investigation shown in the following tables, and while the figures show that the manufacturing interests of the State have not, as yet, reached the former highly prosperous condition, yet, assuming that the amount of money paid out to the wage-earner is a true barometer from which to draw inferences as to the exact industrial situation, conditions are slowly but surely approaching the normal stage of success and prosperity which prevailed throughout the State during the years preceding the period of depression from which the people of Connecticut have so long been suffering.

Concerning the table which shows the increase or decrease in number of persons employed and the ratio of amount disbursed as wages for the three periods of 1896–7–8, in the several localities considered in the tabulation, it should be understood that the number of establishments, the number employed or the amount paid in wages does not include all manufactories or establishments in the specified localities, but only those, the data from which was at hand in the office of the Bureau, with which to make comparisons. Therefore, in the event that the amount shown as having been paid in wages in 1898 should appear as being less than in a previous year, it by no means follows that a less amount has been disbursed in the entire community, but in those establishments only to which the table has reference.

It should be added further, as regards the number employed, that, as is shown by the tables, the number of persons on the pay-rolls of the several establishments on the specified date of July 1st is taken as the basis for the computation, and it must not be inferred that the number so specified is the actual or average number for the year, for by the method above described it is rendered possible to show the number of employes to have been less in 1898 than in a previous year, while the amount disbursed as wages is shown to have been materially in excess of the amount paid out by the same establishments during the preceding year.

INDUSTRY: BRASS AND BRASS GOODS.

Number of Establishment.	Persons employed July 1.		Per cent. number employed.		Amount paid in wages during year ending July 1.		Per cent. amount paid in wages.		Estimated per cent. business done of full capacity.
	1897.	1898.	Increase.	Decrease.	1897.	1898.	Increase.	Decrease.	
1	427	497	16.4	....	$180,500	$221,332	22.6	....	100
2	650	800	23.1	....	316,557	385,000	21.6	....	100
3	60	50	....	16.7	21,000	26,899	28.1	....	75
4	157	164	4.5	....	86,735	95,755	10.4	....	70
5	70	60	....	14.3	32,494	31,200	....	4.	70
6	234	207	....	11.5	100,909	104,080	3.1	....	75
7	716	834	16.5	....	388,523	468,217	20.5	....	100
8	201	187	....	7.	85,504	82,504	....	3.3	70
9	109	112	2.7	....	34,252	36,452	6.4	....	80
10	761	1,005	32.1	....	376,142	521,287	38.1	....	100
11	8	6	....	25.	3,488	2,973	....	14.8	50
12	9	13	44.4	....	4,068	4,856	19.3	....	85
13	220	226	2.7	....	111,971	117,639	5.1	....	80
14	26	25	....	3.8	11,368	10,844	....	4.6	85
15	13	13	....	....	5,067	5,280	4.2	....	70
16	12	13	8.3	....	10,000	10,343	3.4	....	75
17	86	76	....	11.9	46,269	44,188	....	4.5	98
18	8	8	....	....	3,100	3,100	....	....	70
19	6	5	....	16.6	2,000	2,600	30.	....	90
20	533	559	4.9	....	249,195	129,329	....	48.1	60
21	268	250	....	6.7	129,254	143,787	11.2	....	95
22	73	82	12.3	....	37,727	42,218	11.8	....	75
23	118	124	5.1	....	57,691	64,157	11.2	....	85
24	188	200	6.4	....	76,672	81,692	3.8	....	85
25	3	3	....	....	2,260	2,310	2.2	....	75
26	233	240	3.	....	115,575	135,474	17.2	....	100
27	11	7	....	36.3	6,000	3,000	....	50.	30
28	299	226	....	24.4	184,509	141,522	....	23.3	60
29	545	674	23.7	....	244,673	261,714	6.9	....	100
30	10	9	....	10.	3,847	3,809	....	9.	50
31	460	385	....	16.3	219,956	238,307	8.3	....	80

INDUSTRY: BRASS AND BRASS GOODS—*Concluded.*

Number of Establishment.	Persons employed July 1.		Per cent. number employed.		Amount paid in wages during year ending July 1.		Per cent. amount paid in wages.		Estimated per cent. business done of full capacity.
	1897.	1898.	Increase.	Decrease.	1897.	1898.	Increase.	Decrease.	
32	1,461	1,870	28.	....	$742,925	$905,165	21.8	....	100
33	50	56	12.	....	24,000	24,900	3.7	....	80
34	15	13	....	13.3	9,000	5,674	....	36.9	50
35	4	4	....	....	1,680	1,680	....	....	50
36	211	220	4.3	....	105,700	114,705	8.5	....	95
37	169	190	12.4	....	69,965	88,492	26.5	....	67
38	600	653	8.8	....	300,500	351,011	16.8	....	75
39	5	20	300.	....	2,600	5,709	119.6	....	100
40	98	101	3.1	....	57,157	50,384	....	11.8	95
41	321	450	40.2	....	172,615	210,352	21.8	....	100
42	35	40	14.3	....	5,000	18,200	264.	....	100
43	93	85	....	8.6	51,189	48,636	....	5.	50
44	442	496	12.2	....	230,066	282,698	22.9	....	100
45	954	1,272	33.3	....	248,463	576,763	132.1	....	100
46	38	36	....	5.2	20,377	20,351	....	1.	100
47	39	25	....	35.9	16,534	16,185	....	2.1	70
48	83	84	1.2	....	60,986	62,129	1.9	....	100
49	348	450	26.2	....	138,894	236,236	70.1	....	90
50	10	10	....	....	5,825	5,960	2.3	....	75
51	8	14	75.	....	2,184	6,630	203.6	....	100
52	30	34	13.3	....	15,000	16,779	11.9	....	97
53	44	27	....	38.6	17,000	15,373	....	9.6	70
54	150	125	....	16.6	50,000	22,000	....	56.	90
55	612	800	30.7	....	377,044	429,290	13.9	....	100
56	100	135	35.	....	33,556	40,912	21.9	....	85
57	17	21	23.5	....	10,000	12,540	25.4	....	60
58	30	40	33.3	....	14,200	15,000	4.9	....	65
59	21	27	28.5	....	13,000	13,800	6.2	....	25
60	123	130	5.7	....	49,919	59,864	19.9	....	95
61	1,052	1,134	7.8	....	480,184	569,537	18.6	....	90
Total	13,677	15,622	14.2		$6,472,869	$7,648,823	18.2		*89.6

* On basis of wages paid.

INDUSTRY: BUTTONS, BUCKLES AND PINS.

Number of Establishment.	Persons employed July 1.		Per cent. number employed.		Amount paid in wages during year ending July 1.		Per cent. amount paid in wages.		Estimated per cent. business done of full capacity.
	1897.	1898.	Increase.	Decrease.	1897.	1898.	Increase.	Decrease.	
62	70	79	12.9	....	$25,000	$33,000	32.	....	70
63	62	68	9.7	....	24,500	26,000	8.6	....	100
64	22	20	....	9.1	6,755	9,207	36.3	....	80
65	23	24	4.3	....	8,750	9,961	13.8	....	100
66	7	14	100.	....	4,525	1,471	....	67.4	20
67	65	84	27.7	....	17,714	28,262	59.5	....	100
68	84	106	26.1	....	43,710	57,720	32.1	....	80
69	45	52	15.5	....	10,000	14,700	47.	....	80
70	50	65	23.	....	12,500	17,300	38.4	....	100
71	17	17	....	....	7,277	10,742	47.6	....	85
72	12	15	25.	....	3,700	4,805	29.9	....	70
73	300	381	27.	....	140,000	173,300	23.7	....	100
74	263	375	42.6	....	87,643	137,936	57.4	....	100
75	250	250	....	....	75,000	121,019	61.4	....	100
76	99	126	27.1	....	30,815	39,161	27.1	....	85
77	76	84	10.5	....	33,190	32,788	....	1.2	80
Total	1,445	1,760	21.8		$531,079	$717,372	35.1		*92.3

* On basis of wages paid.

INDUSTRY: CARRIAGES AND CARRIAGE PARTS.

Number of Establishment.	Persons employed July 1.		Per cent. number employed.		Amount paid in wages during year ending July 1.		Per cent. amount paid in wages.		Estimated per cent. business done of full capacity.
	1897.	1898.	Increase.	Decrease.	1897.	1898.	Increase.	Decrease.	
78	25	22	....	12.	$15,000	$9,639	....	35.7	60
79	25	25	....	....	11,000	15,000	36.4	....	50
80	32	26	....	18.7	14,397	11,267	....	21.7	20
81	15	15	....	....	14,000	14,200	1.4	....	100
82	13	16	23.1	....	17,996	15,951	....	11.4	70
83	185	200	8.1	....	125,000	128,000	2.4	....	80
84	52	66	26.9	....	35,000	42,000	20.	....	65
85	21	26	23.8	....	15,300	23,677	54.7	....	80
86	100	100	....	....	69,317	69,400	.1	....	75
87	35	40	14.2	....	20,000	17,350	....	13.3	60
88	12	12	....	....	5,600	5,600	....	....	25
89	12	11	....	8.3	8,325	7,449	....	10.5	75
90	3	4	33.3	....	1,800	1,800	....	....	80
91	13	17	30.8	....	5,850	6,665	....	13.9	75
92	27	21	....	22.2	14,200	13,000	....	8.4	50
93	17	15	....	11.8	9,100	8,000	....	12.1	83
94	10	10	....	....	6,200	7,000	12.9	....	80
95	2	2	....	....	1,144	1,144	....	....	50
96	42	40	....	4.8	27,040	26,507	....	1.9	70
97	38	34	....	10.2	15,578	16,418	5.3	....	40
98	22	22	....	....	15,470	15,610	.9	....	100
99	19	20	5.2	....	12,500	13,600	8.8	....	55
Total	720	744	3.3		$459,817	$469,277	2.1		*64.8

* On basis of wages paid.

INDUSTRY: CORSETS.

Number of Establishment.	Persons employed July 1.		Per cent. number employed.		Amount paid in wages during year ending July 1.		Per cent. amount paid in wages.		Estimated per cent. business done of full capacity.
	1897.	1898.	Increase.	Decrease.	1897.	1898.	Increase.	Decrease.	
100	59	60	1.7	....	$14,340	$19,000	32.5	....	85
101	250	250	....	....	85,000	85,000	....	....	85
102	275	300	9.1	....	60,000	66,000	10.	....	90
103	896	934	4.2	....	296,145	332,194	12.2	....	85
104	732	772	5.3	....	215,056	241,597	12.3	....	90
105	205	208	1.4	....	66,269	81,856	23.5	....	95
106	75	91	21.3	....	20,885	26,234	25.6	....	100
107	1,400	1,400	....	....	456,000	510,180	11.9	....	100
108	70	38	....	45.7	15,000	7,703	....	48.6	35
109	380	363	....	4.4	110,000	112,289	2.	....	100
Total	4,342	4,416	1.7		$1,338,695	$1,482,053	10.7		*91.9

* On basis of wages paid.

INDUSTRY: CUTLERY AND TOOLS.

Number of Establishment.	Persons employed July 1.		Per cent. number employed.		Amount paid in wages during year ending July 1.		Per cent. amount paid in wages.		Estimated per cent. business done of full capacity.
	1897.	1898.	Increase.	Decrease.	1897.	1898.	Increase.	Decrease.	
110	46	47	2.1	....	$15,246	$18,395	20.6	....	75
111	5	4	....	20.	3,000	2,500	....	16.6	45
112	22	25	13.6	....	8,300	10,800	30.1	....	85
113	60	50	....	16.6	19,600	25,516	30.2	....	50
114	45	60	33.3	....	17,000	23,409	37.7	....	50
115	70	80	14.3	....	32,000	36,000	12.5	....	30
116	31	34	9.7	....	12,047	15,422	27.1	....	85
117	148	148	....	....	60,629	72,326	19.3	....	33
118	7	13	85.7	....	6,276	5,402	....	13.9	70
119	50	57	14.	....	23,466	23,689	.9	....	95
120	4	4	....	....	1,520	2,037	34.	....	40
121	55	42	....	25.5	31,476	35,506	12.8	....	50
122	75	75	....	....	36,058	39,936	10.9	....	100
123	48	45	....	6.2	14,219	18,888	32.8	....	40
124	120	125	4.2	....	45,000	50,000	11.1	....	100
125	8	9	12.5	....	2,915	3,241	11.2	....	50
126	90	121	34.4	....	46,033	62,580	35.9	....	100
127	99	108	9.1	....	29,324	37,702	21.7	....	90
128	267	320	19.8	....	125,454	130,559	4.1	....	100
129	60	90	50.	....	30,000	40,000	33.3	....	40
130	2	2	....	....	1,350	1,050	....	22.2	40
131	20	20	....	....	10,044	11,681	16.3	....	100
132	5	4	....	20.	2,100	2,000	....	4.7	50
133	14	16	14.3	....	7,540	9,976	32.3	....	65
134	132	201	52.2	....	63,049	84,818	34.5	....	100
135	27	37	37.	....	15,300	11,250	....	26.4	75
136	53	56	5.7	....	25,499	33,263	30.4	....	100
137	106	156	47.2	....	48,255	61,151	50.6	....	95
138	30	34	13.3	....	5,880	11,985	103.8	....	100
139	58	58	....	....	30,852	39,351	27.5	....	100

INDUSTRY: CUTLERY AND TOOLS—*Concluded.*

Number of Establishment.	Persons employed July 1.		Per cent. number employed.		Amount paid in wages during year ending July 1.		Per cent. amount paid in wages.		Estimated per cent. business done of full capacity.
	1897.	1898.	Increase.	Decrease.	1897.	1898.	Increase.	Decrease.	
140	18	17	....	5.5	$16,283	$5,911	....	63.7	50
141	9	8	....	11.1	2,311	2,879	24.6	....	75
142	69	76	10.1	....	34,000	47,500	39.7	....	80
143	4	4	....	....	3,500	4,500	28.5	....	60
144	10	5	....	50.	3,680	1,200	....	67.4	30
145	20	27	35.	....	10,138	13,500	33.2	....	75
Total	1,887	2,178	15.4		$839,344	$995,923	18.7		*67.6

*On basis of wages paid.

INDUSTRY: FIRE ARMS.

Number of Establishment.	Persons employed July 1.		Per cent. number employed.		Amount paid in wages during year ending July 1.		Per cent. amount paid in wages.		Estimated per cent. business done of full capacity.
	1897	1898.	Increase.	Decrease.	1897.	1898.	Increase.	Decrease.	
146	40	55	37.5	....	$19,661	$24,675	25.5	....	100
147	65	68	4.6	....	24,000	35,611	48.4	....	100
148	260	164	....	33.1	130,000	82,637	....	36.4	50
149	7	9	28.6	....	5,600	3,777	....	32.6	20
150	406	611	50.5	....	237,176	301,826	27.2	....	80
151	16	15	....	5.5	7,200	8,500	18.1	....	70
152	12	12	....	....	7,850	8,000	1.9	....	75
Total	806	934	15.9		$431,487	$465,026	7.8		*72.1

* On basis of wages paid.

INDUSTRY: GENERAL HARDWARE.

Number of Establishment.	Persons employed July 1.		Per cent. number employed.		Amount paid in wages during year ending July 1.		Per cent. amount paid in wages.		Estimated per cent business done of full capacity.
	1897.	1898.	Increase.	Decrease.	1897.	1898.	Increase.	Decrease.	
153	12	8	....	33.3	$7,200	$4,000	....	44.4	40
154	49	60	22.4	....	23,281	22,710	....	2.4	75
155	656	765	16.7	....	336,000	373,027	11.	....	85
156	238	233	....	2.1	68,512	68,600	.1	....	70
157	65	60	....	7.6	28,434	36,944	29.9	....	80
158	372	379	1.9	....	150,422	164,190	9.1	....	75
159	7	7	....	....	2,589	2,800	8.1	....	70
160	81	86	6.2	....	33,927	42,940	26.6	....	75
161	50	58	16.	....	20,526	23,210	13.1	....	63
162	41	44	7.3	....	13,122	13,705	4.4	....	70
163	70	79	12.9	....	32,289	29,592	....	8.3	65
164	41	53	29.2	....	13,056	19,012	45.6	....	50
165	14	25	78.5	....	6,969	10,979	57.5	....	75
166	50	50	....	....	18,078	22,430	24.1	....	75
167	60	75	25.	....	24,700	32,000	29.6	....	90
168	413	446	7.9	....	207,343	224,911	8.5	....	58
169	100	100	....	....	50,000	52,800	5.6	....	75
170	35	42	20.	....	20,000	25,000	25.	....	100
171	38	45	18.4	....	20,000	20,000	....	....	80
172	192	187	....	2.6	68,636	86,927	26.6	....	100
173	10	10	....	....	6,257	7,914	26.4	....	75
174	30	30	....	....	14,827	16,679	12.4	....	50
175	13	15	15.4	....	6,458	6,902	6.9	....	65
176	12	22	83.3	....	2,000	2,592	29.6	....	75
177	123	57	....	53.6	49,279	35,567	....	27.8	60
178	83	40	....	51.8	43,393	18,674	....	56.9	30
179	44	44	....	....	19,527	19 387	....	.7	75
180	13	10	....	23.1	3,964	9,215	132.5	....	50
181	135	122	....	9.6	60,000	74,512	24.2	....	90
182	54	66	22.2	....	19,595	23,245	18.6	....	69

INDUSTRY: GENERAL HARDWARE — *Concluded.*

Number of Establishment.	Persons employed July 1.		Per cent. number employed.		Amount paid in wages during year ending July 1.		Per cent. amount paid in wages.		Estimated per cent. business done of full capacity.
	1897.	1898.	Increase.	Decrease.	1897.	1898.	Increase.	Decrease.	
183	276	325	17.7	....	$112,380	$156,015	38.8	....	100
184	36	37	2.8	....	18,704	19,429	3.9	....	45
185	210	206	....	1.9	73,324	82,300	12.2	....	100
186	9	11	22.2	....	4,316	5,000	15.8	....	40
187	21	21	....	....	9,000	10,000	11.1	....	65
188	54	55	1.8	....	19,862	27,073	36.3	....	75
189	36	18	....	50.	8,493	10,254	23.8	....	100
190	205	215	4.7	....	84,048	89,000	5.8	....	100
191	15	18	20.	....	24,354	21,678	....	10.9	90
192	169	183	8.3	....	80,000	89,242	11.6	....	100
193	1,300	1,200	....	7.7	613,836	581,595	....	5.2	80
194	150	175	16.6	....	81,042	72,616	....	10.3	90
195	23	6	....	73.9	10,288	12,000	16.6	....	85
196	15	14	....	6.6	7,500	2,500	....	66.7	25
197	1,093	1,123	2.7	....	413,488	416,000	.6	....	75
198	41	43	4.8	....	22,520	26,538	17.8	....	50
199	168	191	13.7	....	69,000	87,533	26.8	....	95
200	46	45	....	2.2	23,047	23,546	2.2	....	50
201	672	774	15.2	....	250,000	300,000	20.	....	90
202	12	12	....	....	2,700	2,900	7.4	....	50
203	280	279	....	.4	100,000	98,000	....	2.	65
204	70	76	8.6	....	25,000	28,180	12.7	....	75
205	7	34	385.7	....	3,553	8,300	133.3	....	65
206	8	7	....	12.5	3,592	4,193	16.7	....	65
Total	8,017	8,286	3.4		$3,430,431	$3,664,356	6.8		*74.2

* On basis of wages paid.

INDUSTRY: HATS AND CAPS.

Number of Establishment.	Persons employed July 1.		Per cent. number employed.		Amount paid in wages during year ending July 1.		Per cent. amount paid in wages.		Estimated per cent. business done of full capacity.
	1897.	1898.	Increase.	Decrease.	1897.	1898.	Increase.	Decrease.	
207	187	184	....	1.6	$91,500	$102,500	12.1	....	95
208	125	125	....	....	54,757	57,743	5.4	....	55
209	165	205	24.2	....	50,000	56,000	12.	....	100
210	70	75	7.1	....	30,000	30,000	....	....	50
211	125	150	20.	....	48,178	66,998	39.1	....	75
212	69	78	13.	....	43,161	46,151	6.9	....	80
213	40	55	37.5	....	9,000	25,000	188.9	....	100
214	140	144	2.9	....	36,688	44,300	20.7	....	95
215	175	180	2.8	....	50,000	52,000	4.	....	75
216	13	14	7.7	....	12,000	5,000	....	58.3	25
217	201	201	....	....	103,478	64,690	....	37.4	75
218	46	72	56.5	....	28,129	45,664	61.9	....	90
219	304	275	....	9.5	138,443	126,570	....	8.5	70
220	28	32	14.3	....	9,111	12,975	42.4	....	75
221	28	28	....	....	8,763	8,759	....	....	90
222	168	207	23.2	....	79,886	90,124	12.8	....	95
223	254	198	....	22.1	102,600	103,363	.7	....	67
224	60	58	....	3.3	22,000	23,000	4.5	....	68
225	120	115	....	4.2	71,235	71,285	....	....	69
226	42	42	....	....	14,727	7,269	....	50.6	50
227	225	220	....	2.2	103,300	101,027	....	2.2	60
Total	2,585	2,658	2.8		$1,106,956	$1,140,418	3.		*73.5

* On basis of wages paid.

INDUSTRY: IRON AND IRON FOUNDRIES.

Number of Establishment.	Persons employed July 1.		Per cent. number employed.		Amount paid in wages during year ending July 1.		Per cent. amount paid in wages.		Estimated per cent. business done of full capacity.
	1897.	1898.	Increase.	Decrease.	1897.	1898.	Increase.	Decrease.	
228	25	27	8.	....	$14,217	$16,000	12.5	....	65
229	50	80	60.	....	26,000	35,000	34.6	....	100
230	365	432	18.2	....	131,820	169,299	28.5	....	45
231	68	80	17.6	....	36,436	45,500	24.8	....	35
232	100	110	10.	....	48,000	51,323	6.9	....	50
233	71	70	....	1.4	29,818	40,196	34.8	....	75
234	66	94	42.4	....	32,600	43,300	32.8	....	56
235	135	176	30.4	....	68,422	101,830	48.8	....	100
236	517	505	....	2.3	320,000	350,000	9.3	....	85
237	130	106	....	18.4	58,300	54,607	....	6.3	85
238	218	316	44.9	....	125,263	145,846	16.4	....	80
239	6	4	....	33.3	5,000	1,000	....	80.	20
240	300	325	8.3	....	175,000	177,000	1.1	....	85
241	19	21	10.5	....	10,400	12,100	16.3	....	40
242	225	313	39.1	....	170,000	175,000	2.9	....	75
243	25	153	512.	....	70,000	62,000	....	11.4	20
244	41	45	9.7	....	16,800	19,300	14.5	....	40
245	57	51	....	10.5	28,000	22,000	....	21.4	85
246	12	12	....	....	8,639	9,637	11.6	....	60
247	71	80	12.7	....	39,000	42,000	7.7	....	75
248	427	358	....	16.1	208,312	212,061	1.8	....	75
249	40	30	....	25.	23,000	20,000	....	13.1	60
250	30	23	....	29.9	20,593	14,205	....	31.	80
251	10	39	290.	....	6,000	20,195	236.5	....	100
252	13	10	....	23.1	7,538	7,473	....	.9	75
253	40	35	....	12.5	16,000	16,675	4.2	....	100
254	8	8	....	....	3,507	3,492	....	.4	90
255	185	192	3.8	....	124,500	114,700	....	7.8	80

INDUSTRY: IRON AND IRON FOUNDRIES — *Concluded.*

Number of Establishment.	Persons employed July 1.		Per cent. number employed.		Amount paid in wages during year ending July 1.		Per cent. amount paid in wages.		Estimated per cent. business done of full capacity.
	1897.	1898.	Increase.	Decrease.	1897.	1898.	Increase.	Decrease.	
256	175	140	....	20.	$80,000	$70,200	....	12.2	40
257	20	17	... .	15.	11,000	8,317	....	24.4	40
258	35	44	25.7	....	19,567	25,294	29.3	....	50
259	10	6	....	40.	3,600	3,636	1.	....	25
260	28	28	....	....	11,000	11,000	....	....	100
Total	3,522	3,930	11.6		$1,948,332	$2,100,186	7.8		*63.9

* On basis of wages paid.

INDUSTRY: LEATHER GOODS.

Number of Establishment.	Persons employed July 1. 1897.	Persons employed July 1. 1898.	Per cent. number employed. Increase.	Per cent. number employed. Decrease.	Amount paid in wages during year ending July 1. 1897.	Amount paid in wages during year ending July 1. 1898.	Per cent. amount paid in wages. Increase.	Per cent. amount paid in wages. Decrease.	Estimated per cent. business done of full capacity.
261	28	26	....	7.1	$7,385	$10,201	38.1	....	100
262	15	15	....	....	9,979	8,650	....	3.3	25
263	5	5	....	....	3,146	3,146	....	....	70
264	100	97	....	3.	96,320	77,000	....	20.	40
265	30	35	16.6	....	4,000	6,000	50.	....	80
266	17	17	....	....	11,553	11,484	....	.6	70
267	84	80	....	4.7	39,102	41,580	6.3	....	70
268	10	10	....	....	4,580	5,200	13.5	....	60
269	30	29	....	3.3	13,500	16,438	21.8	....	60
270	7	12	71.4	....	5,000	7,800	56.	....	80
271	25	26	4.	....	5,000	12,708	154.2	....	100
272	12	8	....	33.3	3,000	3,047	1.6	....	60
273	55	41	....	25.5	25,000	17,000	....	32.	40
274	150	180	20.	....	69,708	73,714	5.7	....	80
275	15	16	6.6	....	7,200	7,650	6.2	....	75
Total	583	597	2.4		$304,473	$301,618		.9	*56.5

* On basis of wages paid.

INDUSTRY: MACHINE SHOPS.

Number of Establishment.	Persons employed July 1.		Per cent. number employed.		Amount paid in wages during year ending July 1.		Per cent. amount paid in wages.		Estimated per cent. business done of full capacity.
	1897.	1898.	Increase.	Decrease.	1897.	1898.	Increase.	Decrease.	
276	33	36	9.1	....	$25,130	$20,426	....	18.7	50
277	192	281	46.3	....	84,887	110,845	30.6	....	85
278	7	7	....	....	4,200	3,840	....	8.6	90
279	141	223	58.1	....	62,744	91,118	45.2	....	93
280	7	5	....	18.5	4,500	3,665	....	18.5	30
281	48	46	....	4.2	25,150	29,206	16.1	....	55
282	9	8	....	11.1	5,344	5,335	....	.2	60
283	5	4	....	20.	2,470	2,300	....	6.8	60
284	40	32	....	20.	25,448	22,072	....	13.2	70
285	10	8	....	20.	6,500	8,190	26.	....	100
286	26	27	3.8	....	12,956	11,289	....	12.1	80
287	30	38	26.6	....	14,495	15,608	7.6	....	50
288	308	286	....	7.1	164,805	181,700	10.2	....	68
289	6	6	....	....	4,160	5,634	35.4	....	75
290	1,012	1,022	.9	....	638,879	655,108	2.5	....	75
291	25	36	44.	....	19,563	19,000	....	2.9	50
292	106	135	27.3	....	60,000	57,600	....	4.	95
293	12	8	....	33.3	2,924	3,644	24.6	....	65
294	23	20	....	13.	12,676	11,947	....	5.7	70
295	6	5	....	16.6	3,640	2,000	....	45.1	25
296	57	80	40.3	....	35,000	50,000	14.3	....	100
297	19	19	....	....	7,852	14,116	79.8	....	50
298	9	9	....	....	5,000	5,000	....	....	50
299	13	14	7.7	....	8,400	9,000	7.1	....	100
300	12	13	8.3	....	6,375	7,280	14.2	....	60
301	125	145	24.	....	90,187	95,099	5.4	....	100
302	20	47	135.	....	14,866	20,600	38.5	....	65
303	90	80	....	11.1	57,715	51,340	....	11.	70
304	55	50	....	9.1	20,824	22,000	5.6	....	75
305	3	3	....	....	4,334	2,930	....	32.4	50

INDUSTRY: MACHINE SHOPS—*Continued.*

Number of Establishment.	Persons employed July 1.		Per cent. number employed.		Amount paid in wages during year ending July 1.		Per cent. amount paid in wages.		Estimated per cent. business done of full capacity.
	1897.	1898.	Increase.	Decrease.	1897.	1898.	Increase.	Decrease.	
306	2	2	....	....	$1,549	$1,500	....	3.1	25
307	361	398	10.2	....	229,834	232,025	.9	....	90
308	8	12	50.	....	5,500	6,700	21.8	....	65
309	8	10	25.	....	2,650	2,540	....	4.1	50
310	10	10	....	....	10,000	10,000	....	....	50
311	26	25	....	3.8	15,687	16,770	6.9	....	75
312	12	10	....	16.6	8,750	7,500	....	14.2	70
313	20	25	25.	....	8,100	12,000	48.1	....	75
314	97	109	12.4	....	46,000	51,214	11.3	....	75
315	15	17	13.3	....	5,000	7,000	40.	....	85
316	88	90	2.2	....	57,167	66,037	15.5	....	100
317	19	30	57.9	....	27,037	38,000	40.5	....	65
318	60	79	31.7	....	29,610	30,868	4.2	....	100
319	106	115	8.5	....	60,433	62,730	3.8	....	70
320	4	3	....	25.	2,100	1,950	....	7.1	50
321	34	54	58.8	....	14,898	27,158	82.3	....	90
322	333	191	....	42.6	267,319	255,181	....	4.5	100
323	1,007	681	....	32.4	578,000	867,427	50.	....	100
324	213	156	....	26.7	106,730	108,690	1.8	....	100
325	855	853	....	.2	509,606	513,795	.8	....	80
326	18	26	44.4	....	11,992	19,212	60.2	....	100
327	50	60	20.	....	25,711	30,395	18.2	....	100
328	47	50	6.4	....	25,000	29,000	16.	....	75
329	7	6	....	14.3	4,147	3,718	....	10.3	65
330	50	37	....	26.	15,000	22,000	46.6	....	40
331	48	50	4.2	....	19,789	17,198	....	13.1	70
332	61	70	14.7	....	32,091	18,426	....	42.5	78
333	16	19	18.7	....	4,411	7,000	58.6	....	75
334	54	36	....	33.3	31,200	19,424	....	37.7	25
335	1,269	1,158	....	8.7	603,582	725,406	20.2	....	100

INDUSTRY: MACHINE SHOPS—*Concluded.*

Number of Establishment.	Persons employed July 1.		Per cent. number employed.		Amount paid in wages during year ending July 1.		Per cent. amount paid in wages.		Estimated per cent. business done of full capacity.
	1897.	1898.	Increase.	Decrease.	1897.	1898.	Increase.	Decrease.	
336	87	75	....	13.8	$56,594	$44,578	....	21.2	40
337	106	100	....	5.6	43,398	48,037	10.7	....	70
338	6	5	....	16.6	2,083	1,968	....	5.5	50
339	15	12	....	20.	13,000	10,000	....	23.1	25
340	54	57	5.6	....	36,611	38,100	4.1	....	85
341	100	100	....	....	50,000	62,000	24.	....	100
Total	7,715	7,424		3.8	$4,391,603	$5,253,426	19.6		*91.6

*On basis of wages paid.

INDUSTRY: MUSICAL INSTRUMENTS AND PARTS.

Number of Establishment.	Persons employed July 1.		Per cent. number employed.		Amount paid in wages during year ending July 1.		Per cent. amount paid in wages.		Estimated per cent. business done of full capacity.
	1897.	1898.	Increase.	Decrease.	1897.	1898.	Increase.	Decrease.	
342	225	230	2.2	....	$95,409	$96,300	.9	....	50
343	45	40	....	11.1	25,200	18,780	....	25.5	25
344	7	8	14.3	....	3,600	3,700	2.8	....	60
345	163	205	25.7	....	77,857	100,989	29.7	....	100
346	8	8	....	....	3,500	3,600	2.8	....	100
347	302	352	16.5	....	121,634	158,438	30.2	....	100
348	50	50	....	....	25,712	30,622	19.1	....	95
Total	800	893	11.6		$352,912	$412,429	16.9		*72.5

* On basis of wages paid.

INDUSTRY: PAPER AND PAPER GOODS.

Number of Establishment.	Persons employed July 1.		Per cent. number employed.		Amount paid in wages during year ending July 1.		Per cent. amount paid in wages.		Estimated per cent. business done of full capacity.
	1897.	1898.	Increase.	Decrease.	1897.	1898.	Increase.	Decrease.	
349	18	21	16.6	....	$8,079	$11,098	37.3	....	75
350	52	49	....	5.7	10,741	11,698	8.9	....	80
351	45	43	....	4.4	16,386	15,836	....	3.3	67
352	7	7	....	....	2,593	2,593	....	....	30
353	160	145	....	9.4	56,974	58,172	2.1	....	50
354	22	20	....	9.1	8,249	8,688	5.2	....	99
355	44	42	....	4.5	13,600	13,700	.7	....	67
356	70	70	....	....	30,000	24,400	....	18.7	85
357	144	144	....	....	59,535	70,000	17.6	....	75
358	32	32	....	....	15,284	15,691	2.6	....	75
359	48	52	8.3	....	25,660	26,439	3.	....	100
360	16	16	....	....	7,376	6,725	....	8.8	92
361	23	25	8.7	....	7,500	10,000	33.3	....	100
362	187	187	....	....	70,183	70,183	....	....	50
363	35	35	....	....	19,520	16,872	....	13.5	75
364	25	20	....	20.	7,500	6,500	....	13.3	60
365	9	7	....	22.2	5,500	5,000	....	9.1	85
366	480	480	....	....	200,676	195,000	....	2.8	75
367	45	43	....	4.4	13,500	25,000	85.2	....	100
368	30	39	30.	....	9,215	12,349	34.	....	75
369	14	14	....	....	2,500	2,500	....	....	75
370	76	76	....	....	25,000	25,000	....	....	75
371	47	50	6.6	....	18,000	19,736	9.6	....	80
372	9	14	55.5	....	3,500	5,035	43.8	....	75
373	10	12	20.	....	4,200	3,464	....	17.5	50
374	68	56	....	17.6	21,992	21,595	....	1.8	65
375	41	53	29.3	....	16,144	12,641	....	21.7	75
376	7	7	....	....	2,374	3,086	29.9	....	100
377	22	13	....	40.9	4,370	4,346	....	.5	85
378	7	8	14.3	....	2,990	3,003	.4	....	90

INDUSTRY: PAPER AND PAPER GOODS—*Concluded.*

Number of Establishment.	Persons employed July 1.		Per cent. number employed.		Amount paid in wages during year ending July 1.		Per cent. amount paid in wages.		Estimated per cent. business done of full capacity.
	1897.	1898.	Increase.	Decrease.	1897.	1898.	Increase.	Decrease.	
379	13	12	....	7.7	$3,577	$4,867	36.1	....	50
380	7	5	....	28.5	1,722	1,696	....	1.5	85
381	90	90	....	....	39,000	40,000	2.6	....	90
382	10	10	....	....	4,479	4,348	....	2.9	100
383	17	19	11.8	....	6,800	7,500	10.2	....	67
384	62	62	....	....	36,000	30,000	....	16.7	75
385	3	2	....	33.3	475	750	57.9	....	33
386	30	30	....	....	7,500	8,200	9.3	....	50
387	19	26	36.8	....	10,900	14,000	28.8	....	100
388	24	24	....	....	10,000	10,000	....	....	70
389	12	18	50.	....	6,730	7,274	8.1	....	89
390	40	40	....	....	10,000	13,206	32.	....	90
391	30	33	10.	....	10,700	11,290	5.5	....	85
392	7	12	71.4	....	2,593	5,000	92.8	....	50
393	63	75	19.	....	20,039	24,258	21.1	....	75
394	22	15	....	31.8	15,363	14,139	....	7.9	70
395	17	17	....	....	5,100	5,700	11.8	....	50
396	90	86	....	4.4	30,000	31,898	6.3	....	100
397	68	64	....	5.9	22,283	22,563	1.2	....	100
Total	2,417	2,420	.1		$932,402	$962,989	3.3		*71.8

* On basis of wages paid.

INDUSTRY: RUBBER GOODS.

Number of Establishment.	Persons employed July 1.		Per cent. number employed.		Amount paid in wages during year ending July 1.		Per cent. amount paid in wages.		Estimated per cent. business done of full capacity.
	1897.	1898.	Increase.	Decrease.	1897.	1898.	Increase.	Decrease.	
398	64	60	....	6.2	$27,700	$26,000	....	6.1	70
399	292	298	2.1	....	226,462	237,068	4.7	....	100
400	33	162	390.9	....	21,492	70,000	225.7	....	100
401	205	225	9.8	....	77,551	88,000	13.5	....	80
402	30	39	30.	....	11,957	15,682	31.2	....	95
403	115	135	17.4	....	57,500	65,000	13.	....	60
404	1,233	1,298	5.2	....	450,045	642,050	42.7	....	100
405	1,500	1,400	....	6.6	511,218	736,666	44.1	....	100
406	18	11	....	38.8	4,500	6,000	33.3	....	100
407	15	14	....	6.7	7,500	5,013	....	33.2	25
408	250	263	5.2	....	50,000	54,320	8.6	....	100
409	32	39	21.9	....	19,275	21,893	13.6	....	35
410	236	236	....	....	105,466	109,831	4.1	....	65
411	45	75	66.6	....	20,667	34,647	67.6	....	100
Total	4,068	4,255	4.6		$1,591,333	$2,112,170	32.7		*91.7

* On basis of wages paid.

INDUSTRY: SHOES.

Number of Establishment.	Persons employed July 1.		Per cent. number employed.		Amount paid in wages during year ending July 1.		Per cent. amount paid in wages.		Estimated per cent. business done of full capacity.
	1897.	1896.	Increase.	Decrease.	1897.	1896.	Increase.	Decrease.	
412	137	194	41.6	....	$40,000	$49,218	23.	....	100
413	61	60	....	1.6	26,600	22,948	....	13.7	50
414	100	50	....	50.	49,187	10,200	....	79.3	25
415	7	9	28.5	....	4,000	5,000	25.	....	60
416	34	34	....	....	14,339	13,743	....	4.1	85
417	35	44	25.7	....	5,822	22,786	291.4	....	100
418	10	10	....	....	3,500	3,500	....	....	75
419	75	60	....	20.	30,000	30,000	....	....	100
420	75	71	....	5.3	30,000	27,000	....	10.	70
Total	534	532		.4	$203,448	$184,395		9.4	*71.9

* On basis of wages paid.

INDUSTRY: SILVER AND PLATED WARE.

Number of Establishment.	Persons employed July 1.		Per cent. number employed.		Amount paid in wages during year ending July 1.		Per cent. amount paid in wages.		Estimated per cent. business done of full capacity.
	1897.	1896.	Increase.	Decrease.	1897.	1898.	Increase.	Decrease.	
421	217	229	5.5	....	$118,544	$129,282	9.1	....	65
422	20	20	....	....	7,659	10,999	43.6	....	100
423	23	25	8.7	....	11,082	17,500	57.9	....	75
424	66	70	6.1	....	31,625	40,364	27.6	....	90
425	8	4	....	50.	3,900	2,726	....	30.1	75
426	113	103	....	8.8	57,494	55,795	....	3.	75
427	29	44	51.7	....	14,099	18,230	29.3	....	55
428	220	251	14.1	....	77,938	88,230	13.2	....	70
429	80	80	....	....	44,579	88,516	....	13.6	67
430	180	180	....	....	80,376	90,349	12.4	....	90
431	882	915	3.7	....	425,607	492,344	15.6	....	65
432	540	553	2.4	....	267,279	315,328	17.9	....	80
433	95	100	5.2	....	51,599	52,781	2.3	....	65
434	74	80	8.1	....	31,030	34,100	9.9	....	55
435	200	250	25.	....	94,154	111,000	17.9	....	85
436	72	50	....	30.6	25,251	18,514	....	26.6	75
437	125	100	....	20.	52,000	50,000	....	3.8	65
438	128	129	.8	....	62,557	62,449	....	.2	75
439	114	121	6.1	....	58,000	60,000	3.4	....	80
440	90	100	11.1	....	35,000	40,200	....	14.9	65
441	75	81	8.	....	44,994	47,076	4.6	....	50
442	100	107	7.	....	52,589	53,583	1.9	....	50
443	12	9	....	25.	7,200	3,900	....	45.8	33
444	15	30	100.	....	7,570	11,870	58.6	....	100
445	95	50	....	47.4	54,500	50,000	....	8.3	70
446	120	190	58.3	....	64,204	98,100	52.8	....	100
447	215	212	....	1.4	89,235	100,750	12.9	....	65
Total	3,908	4,083	4.5		$1,870,065	$2,093,986	12.		*70.5

* On basis of wages paid.

INDUSTRY: STONE CUTTING AND QUARRYING.

Number of Establishment.	Persons employed July 1.		Per cent. number employed.		Amount paid in wages during year ending July 1.		Per cent. amount paid in wages.		Estimated per cent. business done of full capacity.
	1897.	1898.	Increase.	Decrease.	1897.	1898.	Increase.	Decrease.	
448	2	2	....	....	$800	$800	....	....	25
449	25	25	....	....	9,262	10,742	15.9	....	100
450	302	440	45.7	....	87,937	243,359	176.8	....	75
451	5	3	....	40.	2,576	1,680	....	34.7	80
452	12	10	....	16.6	9,500	4,750	....	50.	80
453	151	130	....	13.9	45,612	40,997	....	10.1	33
454	207	43	....	79.2	63,032	50,791	....	19.2	86
455	21	20	....	4.8	9,133	9,283	1.6	....	90
456	5	9	80.	....	4,300	7,020	63.3	....	85
457	12	9	....	25.	7,200	5,000	....	30.6	65
Total	742	691		6.9	$239,352	$374,422	56.4		*67.3

* On basis of wages paid.

INDUSTRY: WIRE AND WIRE GOODS.

Number of Establishment.	Persons employed July 1.		Per cent. number employed.		Amount paid in wages during year ending July 1.		Per cent. amount paid in wages.		Estimated per cent. business done of full capacity.
	1897.	1898.	Increase.	Decrease.	1897.	1898.	Increase.	Decrease.	
458	3	3	....	....	$1,609	$2,000	24.3	....	67
459	4	4	....	....	1,500	3,500	133.3	....	100
460	60	60	....	....	16,797	17,000	1.2	....	95
461	15	15	....	....	7,042	6,000	....	14.8	45
462	146	161	10.3	....	74,052	71,071	....	4.	90
463	3	3	....	....	1,400	1,400	....	....	75
464	206	256	24.3	....	87,736	115,714	31.9	....	75
465	100	100	....	....	30,000	34,215	10.7	....	55
466	125	125	....	....	53,000	52,000	....	1.8	100
467	18	13	....	27.7	7,200	7,662	6.4	....	60
468	30	34	13.3	....	15,175	20,170	32.9	....	100
Total	710	774	9.		$295,511	$330,732	11.9		*78.7

* On basis of wages paid.

INDUSTRY: WOOD-WORKING.

Number of Establishment.	Persons employed July 1.		Per cent. number employed.		Amount paid in wages during year ending July 1.		Per cent. amount paid in wages.		Estimated per cent. business done of full capacity.
	1897.	1898.	Increase.	Decrease.	1897.	1898.	Increase.	Decrease.	
469	34	41	20.6	....	$25,789	$22,052	....	14.4	75
470	67	50	....	25.4	36,500	35,000	....	4.1	60
471	30	22	....	26.6	12,500	12,000	....	4.	90
472	30	30	....	....	7,453	8,490	13.9	....	40
473	20	21	5.	....	9,000	15,000	66.7	....	100
474	98	100	2.	....	32,100	33,000	2.8	....	75
475	50	20	....	60.	26,000	13,500	....	48.1	60
476	35	45	28.6	....	18,200	25,000	31.9	....	100
477	12	12	....	....	7,020	7,696	9.6	....	100
478	5	5	....	....	2,248	2,223	....	1.1	25
479	15	20	33.3	....	7,500	10,000	33.3	....	66
480	30	33	10.	....	15,722	18,124	15.3	....	90
481	145	170	17.2	....	80,239	77,649	....	3.2	70
482	6	6	....	....	3,952	4,000	1.2	....	75
483	10	10	....	....	4,500	8,000	77.8	....	50
484	20	15	....	25.	19,000	14,000	....	26.3	33
485	18	14	....	27.7	9,163	8,100	....	11.6	50
486	25	36	44.	....	6,623	11,871	79.2	....	80
487	10	51	410.	....	1,837	23,000	1152.	....	100
488	52	32	....	38.5	20,000	13,500	....	32.5	50
489	8	8	....	....	4,500	4,457	....	1.	65
490	6	3	....	50.	2,109	1,000	....	52.5	25
491	49	20	....	59.1	16,255	14,911	....	8.3	85
492	2	2	....	....	950	1,760	85.3	....	20
493	28	29	3.5	....	13,823	17,941	29.8	....	80
494	112	89	....	20.5	50,741	65,890	29.9	....	100
495	52	54	3.8	....	34,628	33,494	....	3.3	75
496	14	14	....	....	4,200	4,300	2.4	....	75
497	6	3	....	50.	3,000	3,500	16.6	....	85
498	9	8	....	11.1	8,000	10,000	25.	....	100

INDUSTRY: WOOD-WORKING—*Concluded.*

Number of Establishment.	Persons employed July 1.		Per cent. number employed.		Amount paid in wages during year ending July 1.		Per cent. amount paid in wages.		Estimated per cent. business done of full capacity.
	1897.	1898.	Increase.	Decrease.	1897.	1898.	Increase.	Decrease.	
499	23	25	8.7	....	$12,175	$18,885	55.1	....	50
500	18	24	33.3	....	11,000	16,928	53.9	....	100
501	56	58	3.6	....	31,000	31,000	....	....	100
502	35	26	....	25.7	15,600	12,596	....	19.2	50
503	433	430	....	.7	159,338	188,440	18.2	....	100
504	4	5	25.	....	1,400	2,038	45.6	....	75
505	245	320	30.6	....	99,117	153,422	54.8	....	60
506	55	20	....	63.6	16,507	12,289	....	25.5	70
507	23	23	....	....	7,020	9,332	32.9	....	75
508	28	32	14.3	....	27,954	11,060	....	60.4	50
509	30	25	....	16.6	20,000	15,000	....	25.	55
510	20	45	125.	....	6,647	11,428	71.9	....	50
Total	1,968	1,996	1.4		$891,310	$1,001,876	12.4		*72.3

* On basis of wages paid.

INDUSTRY: MISCELLANEOUS.

Number of Establishment.	Persons employed July 1.		Per cent. number employed.		Amount paid in wages during year ending July 1.		Per cent. amount paid in wages.		Estimated per cent. business done of full capacity.
	1897.	1898.	Increase.	Decrease.	1897.	1898.	Increase.	Decrease.	
511	17	12	....	29.4	$3,914	$7,150	82.7	....	100
512	35	36	2.8	....	14,097	18,707	32.7	....	100
513	24	22	....	8.3	8,700	8,919	2.5	....	25
514	48	35	....	27.1	14,000	12,000	....	14.3	75
515	4	4	....	....	1,184	1,663	40.4	....	75
516	30	26	....	13.3	25,000	15,642	....	37.4	50
517	30	23	....	23.3	13,864	15,283	10.2	....	75
518	10	9	....	10.	3,666	5,658	54.3	....	75
519	13	13	....	....	6,000	8,000	33.3	....	100
520	14	14	....	....	12,456	11,602	....	6.8	80
521	21	29	38.1	....	8,750	11,600	32.6	....	20
522	9	9	....	....	6,086	6,136	.8	....	75
523	40	36	....	10.	29,328	29,640	1.1	....	100
524	64	65	1.6	....	34,000	33,000	....	2.9	85
525	15	16	6.6	....	3,900	4,500	15.4	....	50
526	5	6	20.	....	2,500	2,500	....	....	50
527	23	25	8.7	....	13,447	14,184	5.5	....	66
528	16	14	....	12.5	6,342	6,815	7.4	....	80
529	39	37	....	5.1	31,000	27,568	....	11.1	75
530	22	20	....	9.1	15,390	16,700	8.5	....	80
531	186	173	....	6.9	100,270	120,000	19.6	....	100
532	22	18	....	18.2	6,920	6,866	....	.8	66
533	20	21	....	5.	12,711	11,113	....	12.6	90
534	20	15	....	25.	9,000	8,000	....	11.1	90
535	17	17	....	....	7,067	7,662	8.4	....	25
536	14	20	14.5	....	6,057	7,550	24.6	....	100
537	29	30	3.4	....	9,768	17,000	74.	....	75
538	57	56	....	1.7	26,000	31,200	20.	....	95
539	13	13	....	....	5,800	6,000	3.4	....	100
540	6	6	....	....	2,335	2,437	4.2	....	70

INDUSTRY: MISCELLANEOUS—*Concluded.*

Number of Establishment.	Persons employed July 1.		Per cent. number employed.		Amount paid in wages during year ending July 1.		Per cent. amount paid in wages.		Estimated per cent. business done of full capacity.
	1897.	1898.	Increase.	Decrease.	1897.	1898.	Increase.	Decrease.	
541	9	10	11.1	....	$5,123	$5,252	2.5	....	80
542	31	36	16.3	....	19,500	22,665	16.2	....	75
543	18	18	....	....	7,643	2,262	....	70.4	90
544	8	11	....	....	6,300	8,000	27.	....	50
545	11	7	....	36.3	3,475	1,769	....	49.1	20
546	14	14	....	....	5,000	5,000	....	....	100
547	25	20	....	20.	8,000	8,000	....	....	60
548	68	67	....	1.4	28,336	32,408	14.3	....	100
549	3	3	....	....	1,825	1,825	....	....	25
550	25	36	44.	....	11,000	16,000	45.5	....	100
551	87	87	....	....	29,918	30,878	3.2	....	75
552	27	28	3.7	....	11,494	12,780	11.2	....	85
553	95	101	6.3	....	62,500	67,600	8.2	....	90
554	6	6	....	....	2,925	2,972	1.6	....	50
555	16	16	....	....	9,000	9,000	....	....	90
556	10	10	....	....	4,000	4,000	....	....	80
557	15	12	....	20.	6,700	3,250	....	51.5	50
558	72	68	....	5.5	25,572	29,573	15.6	....	50
559	10	10	....	....	5,200	1,500	....	71.2	33
560	19	19	....	....	5,285	6,241	18.1	....	90
561	12	13	8.3	....	4,705	6,217	32.1	....	65
562	20	20	....	....	11,812	11,800	....	.1	90
563	17	16	....	5.8	9,000	9,000	....	....	40
564	30	28	....	6.7	15,000	14,100	....	6.	75
Total	1,511	1,476		2.3	$738,865	$787,182	6.5		*72.5

* On basis of wages paid.

RECAPITULATION.

Industry.	Number of Establishments reporting.	Persons employed July 1.		Per cent. number employed.		Amount paid in wages during year ending July 1.		Per cent. amount paid in wages.		Estimated per cent. business done of full capacity on basis of wages paid.
		1897.	1898.	Increase.	Decrease.	1897.	1898.	Increase.	Decrease.	
Brass and Brass Goods.	61	13,667	15,622	14.2	....	$6,472,869	$7,648,823	18.2	....	89.6
Buttons, Buckles and Pins	16	1,445	1,760	21.8	....	531,079	717,372	35.1	....	92.3
Carriages and Carriage Parts	22	720	744	3.3	....	459,817	469,277	2.1	....	64.8
Corsets	10	4,342	4,416	1.7	....	1,338,695	1,482,053	10.7	....	91.9
Cutlery and Tools	36	1,887	2,178	15.4	....	839,344	995,923	18.7	....	67.6
Fire Arms	7	806	934	15.9	....	431,487	465,026	7.8	....	72.1
General Hardware	54	8,017	8,286	3.4	....	3,430,431	3,664,356	6.8	....	74.2
Hats and Caps	21	2,585	2,658	2.8	....	1,106,956	1,140,418	3.	....	73.5
Iron and Iron Foundries	33	3,522	3,930	11.6	....	1,948,332	2,100,186	7.8	....	63.9
Leather Goods	15	583	597	2.4	....	304,473	301,618	....	.9	56.5
Machine Shops	66	7,715	7,424	....	3.8	4,391,603	5,253,426	19.6	....	91.6
Musical Instruments and Parts	7	800	893	11.6	....	352,912	412,429	16.9	....	72.5
Paper and Paper Goods	49	2,417	2,420	.1	....	932,402	962,989	3.3	....	71.8
Rubber Goods	14	4,068	4,255	4.6	....	1,591,333	2,112,170	32.7	....	91.7
Shoes	9	534	532	....	.4	203,448	184,395	....	9.4	71.9
Silver and Plated Ware	27	3,908	4,083	4.5	....	1,870,065	2,093,986	12.	....	70.5
Stone-cutting and Quarrying	10	742	691	....	6.9	239,352	374,422	56.4	....	67.3
Wire and Wire Goods	11	710	774	9.	....	295,511	330,732	11.9	....	78.7
Wood-working	42	1,968	1,996	1.4	....	891,310	1,001,876	12.4	....	72.3
Miscellaneous	54	1,511	1,476	....	2.3	738,865	787,182	6.5	....	72.5
Total	564	61,957	65,669	6.		$28,370,284	$32,498,659	14.6		79.9

STATISTICS OF MANUFACTURES.

The statistical presentations contained in this chapter of the report are based upon the returns made by 564 identical establishments for each of the years 1897 and 1898, and presents a clear statement of the condition of manufactures in the State.

The total number of persons on the pay-rolls of all establishments considered on July 1, 1898, was reported as being 65,669, an increase of six per cent. over the number reported on the pay-rolls of the same establishments on the same date in 1897. The estimated proportion of business done of full capacity by these establishments, based on the amount paid in wages, during the year 1898 was 79.9 per cent., while in 1897 the proportion was 74 per cent., reached by the same method, and in 1896 the proportion of normal business done by all establishments included in the computation in that year was 79.7 per cent. It should be remembered, however, in making comparisons with previous years that the results above shown bear relation to identical establishments only for the years 1897 and 1898. Comparisons made, therefore, with the figures for 1896 should be predicated upon the results obtained from all establishments, and in the aggregate only.

The total amount disbursed for wages by all establishments during the year ending July 1, 1898, was $32,498,659, an increase of 14.6 per cent. over the amount paid in wages by the same establishments in 1897. Thus it appears that while the number employed increased but 6 per cent., the per cent. of increase in amount paid in wages was in excess of this, which can be explained by stating that the number reported as being employed refers to the specified date of July 1, 1898, and by no means can be considered as the average for the year. Hence it can readily be seen that it is thus rendered possible to show a decrease in number employed and an increase in amount paid in wages, and the reverse can also be equally possible.

BY INDUSTRIES.

BRASS AND BRASS GOODS.

Sixty-one manufacturers of lamps, bells, plumbers' fittings, electrical goods, brass foundries and mills reported as having 15,622 persons on their several pay-rolls on July 1, 1898. On the corresponding date in 1897 there were 13,677 individuals employed by the same establishments, 14.2 per cent. being the increase in number employed in 1898 over 1897. The amount paid in wages during the year ending July 1, 1898, by these establishments, was $7,648,823, an increase of 18.2 per cent. over the previous year. The estimated per cent. business done of full capacity, based on wages paid, was 89.6. Comparisons made with the report of this industry in 1897 show that the 67 establishments which reported to the Bureau in that year did a business of 76 per cent. of full capacity, and in 1896 the reports from the same number of establishments, not identical however, showed a business of 83.5 per cent. of normal capacity.

BUTTONS, BUCKLES AND PINS.

Following the same method, and it is found that in the industry classified as buttons, buckles and pins, that on July 1, 1898, there were 1,760 persons employed in the 16 establishments reporting to the Bureau, this being an increase in number employed by the same establishments on the same date in 1897 of 21.8 per cent. The increase in the amount paid in wages by the identical firms during the year ending July 1, 1898, over the same period in 1897, being 35.1 per cent.; and the proportion of business done in 1898 was 92.3 per cent.; in 1897, 76 per cent.; and in 1896, 77.5 per cent. of full capacity.

CARRIAGES AND CARRIAGE PARTS.

Twenty-two establishments engaged in this industry reported to the Bureau, having on July 1, 1898, 744 persons on their several pay-rolls, an increase over 1897 of 3.3 per cent. The increase in amount paid in wages in 1898 over 1897 was 2.1 per cent.; the proportion of business done in 1898 being 64.8 per cent.; in 1897, 63 per cent.; and in 1896, 72 per cent. of full capacity.

CORSETS.

From the manufacturers of corsets there were ten establishments which made reports to the Bureau, 4,416 being the number on all pay-rolls on July 1, 1898, an increase of 1.7 per cent. in number employed, while the wages paid in 1898 shows an increase of 10.7 per cent. over 1897. The business done of full capacity in 1898 was 91.9 per cent.; in 1897, 63 per cent., and in 1896, 87.6 per cent.

CUTLERY AND TOOLS.

Thirty-six establishments engaged in the manufacture of table and pocket cutlery, machinists' tools, files, etc., reported to the Bureau as having 2,178 persons on their various pay-rolls on July 1, 1898. The same establishments reported in 1897 that on the same date of that year there were 1,887 persons employed, hence the increase in 1898 over 1897 was 15.4 per cent. The increase in the amount paid in wages for the same period was 18.7 per cent.; and 67.6 per cent. of full capacity was the estimated proportion of business done.

FIRE ARMS.

The seven establishments in this industry included in the tabulation, report 934 employes on July 1, 1898, an increase of 15.9 per cent. over the number employed in the same establishments for the corresponding period in 1897. The amount paid in wages increased 7.8 per cent., 72.1 per cent. being the proportion of business done of full capacity on the basis of wages paid. The reports from this industry in 1897 showed 60 per cent. as being the proportion of business done of full capacity, and in 1896 it was 57.3 per cent.

GENERAL HARDWARE.

Classified in the tabulation as general hardware are manufacturers of builders' and furniture hardware, toys, saddlery and harness trimmings. The 54 establishments which reported to the

Bureau had 8,286 persons on all pay-rolls on July 1, 1898. The increase over the corresponding period in 1897 was 3.4 per cent., while the amount paid in wages during the same period increased 6.8 per cent., the per cent. of normal business being 74.2.

HATS AND CAPS.

Twenty-one establishments engaged in the hatting industry reported having 2,658 persons on their several pay-rolls on July 1, 1898, an increase in number employed over the previous year of 2.8 per cent. The increase in amount paid in wages by the same establishments during the same period was 3 per cent.; the proportion of business done of full capacity in 1898 was 73.5 per cent.; in 1897 it was 70 per cent., and in 1896, 75.8 per cent.

IRON AND IRON FOUNDRIES.

The thirty-three concerns classified as manufacturers of iron goods, including iron founders, report 3,930 persons as being employed on July 1, 1898. The percentage of increase was 11.6 over the corresponding date in 1897. The increase in amount paid in wages, however, was but 7.8 per cent.; the proportion of business done was reported as 63.9 per cent. of full capacity. In 1897 this industry showed a business of 69 per cent., and in 1896, 83.6 per cent. of normal capacity.

LEATHER GOODS.

Fifteen manufacturers of leather goods made reports to the Bureau, having 597 persons employed on July 1, 1898, an increase in the number on the pay-rolls of the same establishments on the same date in 1897 of 2.4 per cent. In amount paid in wages a decrease of .9 per cent. was shown; 56.5 per cent. of full capacity was the proportion of business done in 1898. The percentage in 1897 was 65 per cent., and in 1896, 80 per cent.

MACHINE SHOPS.

The number of establishments classified as machine shops which made reports to the Bureau was 66, having 7,424 persons on all pay-rolls on July 1, 1898, as against 7,715 employed by the same concerns on the same date in 1897, a decrease of 3.8 per cent. The amount disbursed as wages by these establishments during the year ending July 1, 1898, however, was $5,253,426, an increase of 19.6 per cent. over the amount paid in wages by the same establishments for the same period in 1897. The proportion of business done in 1898 was reported as being 91.6 per cent. of full capacity; in 1897 this proportion was given as 79, and in 1896, 87 per cent.

MUSICAL INSTRUMENTS AND PARTS.

The seven establishments manufacturing this class of goods reported having 893 employes on July 1, 1898, an increase of 11.6 per cent. over 1897. The increase in amount paid in wages was 16.9 per cent., and the proportion of business done in 1898, 72.5 per cent.; in 1897 this industry reported 70 per cent. as the proportion of business done for that year, and in 1896, 69.4 per cent.

PAPER AND PAPER GOODS.

Forty-nine manufacturers of paper and paper goods reported to the Bureau. The number of employes on the pay-rolls of these establishments on July 1, 1898, was 2,420, an increase of .1 per cent. over the number employed by the same establishments at the corresponding date in 1897, while the amount paid in wages during the year ending July 1, 1898, increased 3.3 per cent. over the amount for the same period in the previous year; 71.8 per cent. of full capacity was the proportion of business done in 1898; in 1897, this was reported as 70, and in 1896, 69.3 per cent.

RUBBER GOODS.

In the rubber industry there were 4,255 persons reported as being on the pay-rolls on July 1, 1898, of the 14 establishments which made reports, this being an increase of 4.6 per cent. over the number reported as being employed by the same establishments at the same date in 1897. The amount paid in wages during the same period increased 32.7 per cent.; and the proportion of business done of full capacity was reported as being 91.7 per cent. in 1898, 72 per cent. in 1897, and 63.7 per cent. in 1896.

SHOES.

Nine manufacturers of shoes made reports, the number of employes on July 1, 1898, being 5.32, a decrease from the number employed by them at the same date in 1897 of .4 per cent. The wages paid by the same establishments, as shown by the returns made, decreased 9.4 per cent. The proportion of business done of full capacity in 1898 was reported as 71.9 per cent.; in 1897, 88 per cent., and in 1896, 83.9 per cent.

SILVER AND PLATED WARE.

Manufacturers of silver and plated ware to the number of 27 reported having 4,083 employes on their several pay-rolls on July 1, 1898, showing an increase over the number employed by the same establishments in 1897 of 4.5 per cent. In amount paid in wages by the identical establishments the increase for the year ending July 1, 1898, over the same period in 1897, was 12 per cent.: 70.5 per cent. of full capacity was the proportion of business reported for 1898; in 1897 it was estimated as being 63 per cent., and in 1896, 73.6 per cent.

STONE-CUTTING AND QUARRYING.

The number of persons reported as being on the pay-rolls of the 10 establishments engaged in this industry on July 1, 1898, was 691, a decrease from the number employed by the same establishments on the same date in 1897 of 6.9 per cent. An increase of 56.4 per cent. was shown in the amount paid in wages by these establishments in the two periods. The proportion of business done of full capacity in 1898 was estimated as being 67.3 per cent.: in 1897, it was 58 per cent., and in 1896, 72.2 per cent.

WIRE AND WIRE GOODS.

The 11 establishments reporting as being engaged in the manufacture of wire and wire goods had 774 persons on their various pay-rolls on July 1, 1898. Nine per cent. was the increase in number employed over the corresponding period in 1897. The increase in amount paid in wages during the same period was 11.9 per cent., and the proportion of business done of full capacity 78.7 per cent. This was reported as being 65 per cent. in 1897, and 78.4 per cent. in 1896.

WOOD-WORKING.

Engaged in this industry there were 42 establishments which made reports, the number employed on July 1, 1898, was stated as being 1,996, an increase in number employed by the same establishments at the same date in 1897 of 1.4 per cent. There was a reported increase of 12.4 per cent. in amount paid in wages in 1898 over the amount paid by the same establishments during the same period in 1897; 72.3 per cent. of full capacity was the estimated proportion of business done in 1898 by all establishments reporting. In 1897 it was reported as being 74 per cent., and in 1896, 76.8 per cent.

MISCELLANEOUS.

By the 54 establishments classified as miscellaneous there were 1,476 persons employed on July 1, 1898, showing a decrease of 2.3 per cent. from the number on the pay-rolls of the same establishments at the same date in 1897. There was, however, an increase of 6.5 per cent. in amount paid in wages by the identical concerns during that period. The proportion of business done of full capacity in 1898 was reported to have been 72.5 per cent.; in 1897 it was 79 per cent., and in 1896, 82.2 per cent.

DIVISION BY LOCALITIES.

Locality.	Number of Estab-lishments reporting.	Persons employed July 1.		Per cent. Increase + Decrease − 1898 compared with		Amount paid in wages during year ending July 1.		Per cent. Increase + Decrease − 1898 compared with	
		1897.	1898.	1896.	1897.	1897.	1898.	1896.	1897.
Ansonia	9	2,250	2,490	+48.2	+10.6	$1,083,583	$1,275,797	+37.5	+17.7
Bridgeport	76	8,693	9,845	+14.	+13.3	3,762,873	4,320,378	−15.2	+14.8
Bristol	17	1,289	1,311	−.1	+1.7	622,237	612,035	+7.	−1.6
Danbury	24	2,076	2,088	+.9	+.6	910,153	893,921	−1.1	−1.8
Hartford	69	6,996	6,916	−6.7	−1.1	4,053,394	4,446,730	+.2	+9.7
Killingly	10	1,002	1,077	+10.9	+7.4	273,697	387,074	+54.4	+41.4
Meriden	28	3,446	3,765	+2.5	+9.3	1,694,368	1,627,421	−1.5	−4.
Middletown	14	1,646	1,764	−8.9	+7.2	563,269	601,077	−7.4	+6.7
New Britain	20	3,859	3,910	−11.6	+1.3	1,534,301	1,667,665	−13.4	+8.7
New Haven	70	5,358	5,408	−4.	+.9	2,279,740	2,646,204	−7.8	+16.1
New London	9	1,441	1,684	+14.2	+16.9	501,114	607,349	+22.8	+21.2
Norwalk	11	1,567	1,626	+8.5	+3.8	561,355	614,137	+11.3	+9.4
Norwich	26	4,155	4,095	−9.2	−1.4	1,441,684	1,527,683	−15.6	+6.
Putnam	12	864	918	+28.3	+6.3	280,727	297,234	+4.1	+5.9
Rockville	11	1,429	1,557	+7.9	+9.	402,662	507,652	+9.1	+26.1
Stafford	12	824	997	+21.	+21.	282,933	367,080	+17.2	+29.7
Stamford	7	1,105	1,358	+18.	+22.9	507,698	583,189	−.3	+14.9
Torrington	6	1,369	1,598	+27.	+16.7	657,088	815,247	+26.4	+24.1
Wallingford	10	1,505	1,667	+16.1	+10.8	722,825	895,900	+22.7	+23.9
Waterbury	44	8,531	9,001	+5.1	+5.5	3,892,248	4,874,117	+11.	+25.2
Willimantic	5	1,817	1,907	+1.4	+5.	573,316	632,569	−11.6	+10.3
Winsted	19	1,211	1,237	+11.4	+2.1	500,620	501,207	+14.2	+.1

DIVISION BY LOCALITIES.

This table is designed to show the increase or decrease of the number of persons employed on July 1, 1897, and July 1, 1898, also the gross amount distributed as wages by the establishments represented, during the two years ending on the dates above given in twenty-two selected cities and towns.

This comparison has reference to the same establishments in all cases. As has been said elsewhere it does not represent all of the establishments of any given locality, only those which have reported being considered.

An analysis shows a gratifying increase in the number of persons employed and the amount of wages distributed. Of the twenty-two localities considered, sixteen show an increase over 1896, and twenty an increase over 1897 in the number of persons employed, Stafford showing the largest, an increase of 21 per cent.

In the distribution of wages thirteen localities show an increase over 1896, and nineteen an increase over 1897. The greatest increase is shown in Killingly, where it is 41 per cent., Stafford following with 29 per cent., and Wallingford 23.9 per cent. But six of the localities considered in 1897 showed an increase over 1896.

PART IV.

LABOR LEGISLATION,

1897-8.

LABOR LEGISLATION.

THREE bills were before the Fifty-fifth Congress which are of interest to organized labor. Two of them, one creating a National Arbitration Board to mediate in disputes between common carriers and their employes, and the other authorizing the "Appointment of a nonpartisan commission" to collate information and to consider and recommend legislation to meet the problems presented by labor, agriculture and capital, were passed. The full text of each is here given:

An Act Concerning Carriers Engaged in Interstate Commerce and Their Employees.

Be it enacted by the Senate and House of Representatives of the United States of America in Congress assembled, That the provisions of this Act shall apply to any common carrier or carriers and their officers, agents, and employees, except masters of vessels and seamen, as defined in section forty-six hundred and twelve, Revised Statutes of the United States, engaged in the transportation of passengers or property wholly by railroad, or partly by railroad and partly by water, for a continuous carriage or shipment, from one State or Territory of the United States, or the District of Columbia, to any other State or Territory of the United States, or the District of Columbia, or from any place in the United States to an adjacent foreign country, or from any place in the United States through a foreign country to any other place in the United States.

The term "railroad" as used in this Act shall include all bridges and ferries used or operated in connection with any railroad, and also all the road in use by any corporation operating a railroad, whether owned or operated under a contract, agreement, or lease; and the term "transportation" shall include all instrumentalities of shipment or carriage.

The term "employees" as used in this Act shall include all persons actually engaged in any capacity in train operation or train service of any description, and notwithstanding that the cars upon or in which they are employed may be held and operated by the carrier under a lease or other contract; Provided, however, That this Act shall not be held to apply to employees of street railroads and shall apply only to employees engaged in railroad train service. In every such case the carrier shall be responsible for the acts and defaults of such employees in the same manner and to the same extent as if said cars were owned by it and said employees directly employed by it, and any provisions to the contrary of any such lease or other contract shall be binding only as between the parties thereto and shall not affect the obligations of said carrier either to the public or to the private parties concerned.

Sec. 2. That whenever a controversy concerning wages, hours of labor, or conditions of employment shall arise between a carrier subject to this Act and the employees of such carrier, seriously interrupting or threatening to interrupt the business of said carrier, the chairman of the Interstate Commerce Commission and the Commissioner of Labor shall, upon the request of either party to the controversy, with all practicable expedition, put themselves in communication with the parties to such controversy, and shall use their best efforts, by mediation and conciliation, to amicably settle the same; and if such efforts shall be unsuccessful, shall at once endeavor to bring about an arbitration of said controversy in accordance with the provisions of this Act.

Sec. 3. That whenever a controversy shall arise between a carrier subject to this Act and the employees of such carrier which can not be settled by mediation and conciliation in the manner provided in the preceding section, said controversy may be submitted to the arbitration of a board of three persons, who shall be chosen in the manner following: One shall be named by the carrier or employer directly interested; the other shall be named by the labor organization to which the employees directly interested belong, or, if they belong to more than one, by that one of them which specially represents employees of the same grade and class engaged in services of the same nature as said employees so directly interested: Provided, however, That when a controversy involves and affects the interests of two or more classes and grades of employees belonging to different labor organizations, such arbitrator shall be agreed upon and designated by the concurrent action of all such labor organizations; and in cases where the majority of such employees are not members of any labor organization, said employees may by a majority vote select a committee of their own number, which committee shall have the right to select the arbitrator on behalf of said employees. The two thus chosen shall select the third commissioner of arbitration; but, in the event of their failure to name such arbitrator within five days after their first meeting, the third arbitrator shall be named by the commissioners named in the preceding section. A majority of said arbitrators shall be competent to make a valid and binding award under the provisions hereof. The submission shall be in writing, shall be signed by the employer and by the labor organization representing the employees, shall specify the time and place of meeting of said board of arbitration, shall state the questions to be decided, and shall contain appropriate provisions by which the respective parties shall stipulate, as follows:

First. That the board of arbitration shall commence their hearings within ten days from the date of the appointment of the third arbitrator, and shall find and file their award, as provided in this section, within thirty days from the date of the appointment of the third arbitrator; and that pending the arbitration the status existing immediately prior to the dispute shall not be changed: Provided, That no employee shall be compelled to render personal service without his consent.

Second. That the award and the papers and proceedings, including the testimony relating thereto certified under the hands of the arbitrators and which shall have the force and effect of a bill of exceptions, shall be filed in the clerk's office of the circuit court of the United States for the district wherein the controversy arises or the arbitration is entered into, and shall be final and conclusive upon both parties, unless set aside for error of law apparent on the record.

Third. That the respective parties to the award will each faithfully execute the same, and that the same may be specifically enforced in equity so far as the powers of a court of equity permit: Provided, That no injunction or other legal process shall be issued which shall compel the performance by any laborer against his will of a contract for personal labor or service.

Fourth. That employees dissatisfied with the award shall not by reason of such dissatisfaction quit the service of the employer before the expiration of three months from and after the making of such award without giving thirty days' notice in writing of their intention so to quit. Nor shall the employer dissatisfied with such award dismiss any employee or employees on account of such dissatisfaction before the expiration of three months from and after the making of such award without giving thirty days' notice in writing of his intention so to discharge.

Fifth. That said award shall continue in force as between the parties thereto for the period of one year after the same shall go into practical operation, and no new arbitration upon the same subject between the same employer and the same class of employees shall be had until the expiration of said one year if the award is not set aside as provided in section four. That as to individual employees not belonging to the labor organization or organizations which shall enter into the arbitration, the said arbitration and the award made therein shall not be binding, unless the said individual employees shall give assent in writing to become parties to said arbitration.

Sec. 4. That the award being filed in the clerk's office of a circuit court of the United States, as hereinbefore provided, shall go into practical operation, and judgment shall be entered thereon accordingly at the expiration of ten days from such filing, unless within such ten days either party shall file exceptions thereto for matter of law apparent upon the record, in which case said award shall go into practical operation and judgment be entered accordingly when such exceptions shall have been finally disposed of either by said circuit court or on appeal therefrom.

At the expiration of ten days from the decision of the circuit court upon exceptions taken to said award, as aforesaid, judgment shall be entered in accordance with said decision unless during said ten days either party shall appeal therefrom to the circuit court of appeals. In such case only such portion of the record shall be transmitted to the appellate court as is necessary to the proper understanding and consideration of the questions of law presented by said exceptions and to be decided.

The determination of said circuit court of appeals upon said questions shall be final, and being certified by the clerk thereof to said circuit court, judgment pursuant thereto shall thereupon be entered by said circuit court.

If exceptions to an award are finally sustained, judgment shall be entered setting aside the award. But in such case the parties may agree upon a judgment to be entered disposing of the subject-matter of the controversy, which judgment when entered shall have the same force and effect as judgment entered upon an award.

Sec. 5. That for the purposes of this Act the arbitrators herein provided for, or either of them, shall have power to administer oaths and affirmations, sign subpoenas, require the attendance and testimony of witnesses, and the production of such books, papers, contracts, agreements, and documents material to a just determination of the matters under investigation as may be ordered by the court; and may invoke the aid of the United States courts to compel witnesses to attend and testify and to produce such books, papers, contracts, agreements and documents to the same extent and under the same conditions and penalties as is provided for in the Act to regulate commerce, approved February fourth, eighteen hundred and eighty-seven, and the amendments thereto.

Sec. 6. That every agreement of arbitration under this Act shall be acknowledged by the parties before a notary public or clerk of a district or circuit court of the United States, and when so acknowledged a copy of the same shall be transmitted to the chairman of the Interstate Commerce Commission, who shall file the same in the office of said commission.

Any agreement of arbitration which shall be entered into conforming to this Act, except that it shall be executed by employees individually instead of by a labor organization as their representative, shall, when duly acknowledged as herein provided, be transmitted to the chairman of the Interstate Commerce Commission, who shall cause a notice in writing to be served upon the arbitrators, fixing a time and place for a meeting of said board, which shall be within fifteen days from the execution of said agreement of arbitration: Provided, however, That the said chairman of the Interstate Commerce Commission shall decline to call a meeting of arbitrators under such agreement unless it be shown to his satisfaction that the employees signing the submission represent or include a majority of all employees in the service of the same employer and of the same grade and class, and that an award pursuant to said submission can justly be regarded as binding upon all such employees.

Sec. 7. That during the pendency of arbitration under this Act it shall not be lawful for the employer, party to such arbitration, to discharge the employees, parties thereto, except for inefficiency, violation of law, or neglect of duty; nor for the organization representing such employees to order, nor for the employees to unite in, aid or abet, strikes against said employer; nor, during a period of three months after an award under such an arbitration, for such employer to discharge any such employees, except for the causes aforesaid, without giving thirty days' written notice of an intent so to discharge; nor for any of such employees, during a like period, to quit the service of said employer without just cause, without giving to said employer thirty days' written notice of an intent so to do; nor for such organization representing such employees to order, counsel, or advise otherwise. Any violation of this section shall subject the offending party to liability for damages: Provided, That nothing herein contained shall be construed to prevent any employer, party to such arbitration, from reducing the number of its or his employees whenever in its or his judgment business necessities require such reduction.

Sec. 8. That in every incorporation under the provisions of chapter five hundred and sixty-seven of the United States Statutes of eighteen hundred and eighty-five and eighteen hundred and eighty-six it must be provided in the articles of incorporation and in the constitution, rules, and by-laws that a member shall cease to be such by participating in or by instigating force or violence against persons or property during strikes, lockouts, or boycotts, or by seeking to prevent others from working through violence, threats, or intimidations. Members of such incorporations shall not be personally liable for the acts, debts, or obligations of the corporations, nor shall such corporations be liable for the acts of members or others in violation of law; and such corporations may appear by designated representatives before the board created by this Act, or in any suits or proceedings for or against such corporations or their members in any of the Federal courts.

Sec. 9. That whenever receivers appointed by Federal courts are in the possession and control of railroads, the employees upon such railroads shall have the right to be heard in such courts upon all questions affecting the terms and conditions of their employment, through the officers and representatives of their associations, whether incorporated or unincorporated, and no reduction of wages shall be made by such receivers without the authority of the court therefor upon notice to such employees, said notice to be not less than twenty days before the hearing upon the receivers' petition or application, and to be posted upon all customary bulletin boards along or upon the railway operated by such receiver or receivers.

Sec. 10. That any employer subject to the provisions of this Act and any officer, agent, or receiver of such employer who shall require any employee, or any persons seeking employment, as a condition of such employment, to enter into an agreement, either written or verbal, not to become or remain a member of any labor corporation, association, or organization; or shall threaten any employee with loss of employment, or shall unjustly discriminate against any employee because of his membership in such a labor corporation, association, or organization; or who shall require any employee or any person seeking employment, as a condition of such employment, to enter into a contract whereby such employee or applicant for employment shall agree to contribute to any fund for charitable, social, or beneficial purposes; to release such employer from legal liability for any personal injury by reason of any benefit received from such fund beyond the proportion of the benefit arising from the employer's contribution to such fund; or who shall, after having discharged an employee, attempt or conspire to prevent such employee from obtaining employment, or who shall, after the quitting of an employee, attempt or conspire to prevent such employee from obtaining employment, is hereby declared to be guilty of a misdemeanor, and, upon conviction thereof in any court of the United States of competent jurisdiction in the district in which such offense was committed, shall be punished for each offense by a fine of not less than one hnudred dollars and not more than one thousand dollars.

Sec. 11. That each member of said board of arbitration shall receive a compensation of ten dollars per day for the time he is actually employed, and his traveling and other necessary expenses; and a sum of money sufficient to pay the same, together with the traveling and other necessary and proper expenses of any conciliation or arbitration had hereunder, not to exceed ten thousand dollars in any one year, to be approved by the chairman of the Interstate Commerce Commission and audited by the proper accounting officers of the Treasury, is hereby appropriated for the fiscal years ending June thirtieth, eighteen hundred and ninety-eight, and June thirtieth, eighteen hundred and ninety-nine, out of any money in the Treasury not otherwise appropriated.

Sec. 12. That the Act to create boards of arbitration or commission for settlingcontroversies and differences betweenrailroad corporations and other common carriers engaged in interstate or territorial transportation of property or persons and their employees, approved October first, eighteen hundred and eighty-eight, is hereby repealed.

Approved, June 1, 1898.

An Act Authorizing the Appointment of a Nonpartisan Commission to Collate Information and to Consider and Recommend Legislation to Meet the Problems Presented by Labor, Agriculture, and Capital.

Be it enacted by the Senate and House of Representatives of the United States of America in Congress assembled, That a commission is hereby created, to be called the "Industrial Commission," to be composed as follows: Five members of the Senate, to be appointed by the presiding officer thereof; five members of the House of Representatives, to be appointed by the Speaker, and nine other persons, who shall fairly represent the different industries and employments, to be appointed by the President, by and with the advice and consent of the Senate.

Sec. 2. That it shall be the duty of this commission to investigate questions pertaining to immigration, to labor, to agriculture, to manufacturing, and to business, and to report to Congress and to suggest such legislation as it may deem best upon these subjects.

Sec. 3. That it shall furnish such information and suggest such laws as may be made a basis for uniform legislation by the various States of the Union, in order to harmonize conflicting interests and to be equitable to the laborer, the employer, the producer, and the consumer.

Sec. 4. That the commission shall give reasonable time for hearings, if deemed necessary, and if necessary it may appoint a subcommission or subcommissions of its own members to make investigation in any part of the United States, and it shall be allowed actual necessary expenses for the same. It shall have the authority to send for persons and papers and to administer oaths and affirmations. All necessary expenses, including clerks, stenographers, messengers, rent for place of meeting, and printing and stationery, shall be paid from any money in the Treasury not otherwise appropriated; however, not to exceed fifty thousand dollars per annum for expenditures under this section.

Sec. 5. That it may report from time to time to the Congress of the United States, and shall at the conclusion of its labors submit a final report.

Sec. 6. That the term of the commission shall be two years. The salary of each member of this commission appointed by the President shall be three thousand six hundred dollars per annum. Each member of the commission shall be allowed actual traveling expenses.

Sec. 7. That any vacancies occurring in the commission by reason of death, disability, or from any other cause shall be filled by appointment by the officer and in the same manner as was the member whose retirement from the commission creates the vacancy. That in case the term of a Senator or Representative expires while a member of this commission, said Senator or Representative shall not thereby cease to be a member of said commission, but shall serve until the expiration of the term for which he was appointed, drawing pay from the time his term as Senator or Representative expires, at the same salary as those members of the commission appointed by the President of the United States.

Sec. 8. That a sum sufficient to carry out the provisions of this Act is hereby appropriated out of any money in the Treasury of the United States not otherwise appropriated.

Approved, June 18, 1898.

A bill to regulate the hours of labor, known as the "Eight Hour Bill," passed in the House, is now before the Senate, with the amendments added by the Senate Committee on Education and Labor, and reported without recommendation. The text of the bill, as it is now written, follows:

55th Congress, Second Session.
H. R. 7389.

Passed the House of Representatives May 17th, 1898,

IN THE SENATE OF THE UNITED STATES.
May 18, 1898.

Read twice and referred to the Committee on Education and Labor.
June 29, 1898.

Reported by Mr. Kyle, with amendments, but without recommendation.

Amended in the Senate Committee by the insertion of the part printed in italics.

AN ACT

Limiting the hours of daily services of laborers, workmen, and mechanics employed upon the public works of, or work done for the United States, or any Territory, or the District of Columbia.

Be it enacted by the Senate and House of Representatives of the United States of America in Congress assembled, That the time of service of all laborers, workmen, and mechanics employed upon any public works of, or work done for the United States, or any Territory, or the District of Columbia, whether said work is done by contract or otherwise, is hereby limited and restricted to eight hours in any one calendar day; and it shall be unlawful for any officer of the United States, or of any Territory, or the District of Columbia, or any person acting for or on behalf of the United States, or any Territory, or said District, or any contractor or subcontractor for any part of any public works of, or work done for the United States, or any Territory, or said

District, or any person whose duty it shall be to employ or to direct and control the services of such laborers, workmen, or mechanics, or who has in fact the direction or control of the services of such laborers, workmen, or mechanics, to require or permit them, or any of them, to labor more than eight hours in any one calendar day, except in cases of extraordinary emergency caused by fire, flood, or danger to life or property, *or except* to work upon public military or naval works or defences in time of war.

Sec. 2. That each and every contract to which the United States, any Territory, or the District of Columbia is a party, and every contract made for or on behalf of the United States, or any Territory, or said District, which contract may involve the employment of laborers, workmen, or mechanics, shall contain a stipulation that no laborer, workmen, or mechanic in the employ of the contractor or any subcontractor doing or contracting to do any part of the work contemplated by the contract, shall be required or permitted to work more than eight hours in any one calendar day, *except in cases of extraordinary emergency caused by fire, flood, or danger to life or property, or except to work upon public, military, or naval works or defenses in time of war*, and each and every such contract shall stipulate a penalty for each violation of the stipulation directed by this Act of ten dollars for each laborer, workman, or mechanic, for each and every calendar day in which he shall labor more than eight hours; and the inspector or other officer or person whose duty it shall be to see that the provisions of any such contract are complied with, shall report to the proper officer of the United States, or any Territory, or the District of Columbia, all violations of the stipulation in this Act, provided for in each and every such contract, and the amount of the penalties stipulated in any such contract shall be withheld by the officer or person whose duty it shall be to pay the moneys due under such contract, whether the violations for which said penalties were imposed were by the contractor, his agents, or employees, or any subcontractor, his agents, or employees. No person on behalf of the United States, or any Territory, or the District of Columbia, shall rebate or remit any penalty imposed under any stipulation herein provided for unless upon a finding which he shall make up and certify that such penalty was imposed by reason of an error of fact.

Sec. 3. That any officer of the United States, or any Territory, or the District of Columbia, or any person acting for or on behalf of the United States, or any Territory, or the District of Columbia, who shall violate the provisions of this Act, shall be deemed guilty of a misdeameanor and be subject to a fine or imprisonment, or both, at the discretion of the court, the fine not to exceed five hundred dollars, nor the imprisonment one year.

Sec. 4. That all acts and parts of acts inconsistent with this Act, in so far as they are inconsistent, be, and the same are hereby, repealed. But nothing in this Act shall apply to any existing contract, or to soldiers and sailors enlisted, respectively, in the Army or Navy of the United States, or to seamen on seagoing vessels, *or to the transportation of mails, merchandise, or passengers, or to common carriers in any way.*

Laws have been enacted during this period in a number of the States relating to labor. The subject of legislation and the State enacting the law is here given.

UNITED STATES.—

Forbidding importation of convict-made goods. Appointing a nonpartisan commission to collate information and recommend legislation to meet labor problems. Appointing a Board of Mediation and Arbitration in disputes between common carriers and their employes.

COLORADO.—

Creating a State Board of Mediation and Arbitration. Forbidding blacklisting and boycotting. Requiring horseshoers to pass an examination and be licensed before practicing their trade.

DISTRICT OF COLUMBIA.—

Requiring plumbers and gas-fitters to pass examination and be licensed before practicing their trade.

ILLINOIS.—

Requiring horseshoers to pass an examination and be licensed before practicing their trade.

KENTUCKY.—

Requiring the payment of wages in cash and making the "truck system" unlawful.

MARYLAND.—

Requiring steam engineers, plumbers and horseshoers to pass an examination and be licensed before practicing their trade.

MASSACHUSETTS.—

Requiring gas-fitters to pass examination and be licensed before practicing their trade. Requiring street railway companies to use vestibule cars.

MINNESOTA.—

Requiring barbers, horseshoers and plumbers to pass examination and be licensed before practicing their trade.

NEBRASKA.—

Requiring street railway companies to use vestibule cars.

NEW JERSEY.—

Requiring street railway companies to use vestibule cars.

NEW YORK.—

A general labor law providing for vestibuled cars on street railways. Eight-hour workday for State employes. Ten-hour workday for service and electric railway and brickyard employes. Weekly payment of wages. Wages of employes to be a preferred claim. Wages to be paid in cash. Providing for examination of scaffoldings used in the erection of buildings. Forbidding the employment of alien laborers on public works.

PENNSYLVANIA.—

Forbidding the employment of women and minors more than sixty hours in any one week. Providing for the inspection of bake-shops. Eight-hour workday for State or municipal employes. Forbidding discharge of an employe for belonging to a labor organization.

VIRGINIA.—

Creating a Bureau of Labor Statistics. Protection of "Trade-Marks" of trade unions. Requiring street railway companies to use vestibuled cars.

WASHINGTON.—

Creating a Bureau of Labor Statistics. Requiring contractors for State, county, municipal or other public works to file a bond that wages of all employes shall be paid. Requiring plumbers to pass an examination and be licensed before practicing their trade.

WISCONSIN.—

Requiring convict-made goods to be branded. Requiring plumbers to pass an examination and be licensed before practicing their trade. Requiring bake-shops to be examined for sanitary conditions.

INDEX.

INDEX.

PART I.

Textile Industries of Connecticut.

Cotton Cloth—

PART II.

Organized Labor in Connecticut.

PART III.

Condition of Manufactures.

PART IV.

Labor Legislation.

Made in United States
Troutdale, OR
11/03/2026

56844504R00133